Stock Market Efficiency

Theory, Evidence and Implications

SIMON M. KEANE

University of Glasgow

Philip Allan

First published 1983 by

PHILIP ALLAN PUBLISHERS LIMITED
MARKET PLACE
DEDDINGTON
OXFORD
OX5 4SE

British Library Cataloguing in Publication Data

Keane, Simon
    Stock market efficiency.
    1. Investment analysis
    I. Title
    332.64'2   HG4521

    ISBN 0-86003-519-0
    ISBN 0-86003-619-7   Pbk

Set by MHL Typesetting Ltd, Coventry
Printed at The Pitman Press, Bath

Contents

iii

Preface

In almost every discipline where there is controversy, a potential conflict exists between the desire to pursue a thoroughly rigorous approach and the desire to achieve a more widespread understanding of the subject matter. No one who is familiar with the literature of efficient market research could deny that in the main its methods are characterised by supremely rigorous and critical thinking. It is no less true, however, that the body of literature that has grown significantly over the last few decades has tended to remain remote and inaccessible to many of those who are most likely to be affected by it. The purpose of this book is to help fill the need for greater awareness of this literature and its significance for stock market agents and participants. The aim, therefore, is to provide a reasonably comprehensive but substantially non-mathematical treatment of the topic. It is hoped that a reasonable balance between rigour and understanding may have been achieved.

The behaviour of the vast majority of stock market participants, professional and lay, informed and ill-informed, appears to be premised entirely on the assumption that market prices 'incorrectly' reflect underlying values with sufficient margin and frequency to justify a policy of actively striving to outperform the market. Side-by-side with this activity is an extensive body of research accumulated over a period of years which, for the main part, conflicts with the practitioner's basic premise and which suggests that the conventional investor in search of mispriced securities is largely a victim of self-deception. As a result, there has been a tendency for views to polarise, those on the one hand who accept market efficiency as an indisputable economic fact of life, and those on the other who either ignore it or reject it as irrelevant to real-world investment issues.

What is perhaps relatively new to the debate is the emergence of a small but growing number of research studies which ostensibly offer some support for the practitioner's claim that the market is fallible and exploitable. It is of course understandable that, when so many of the findings have consistently favoured the efficient market viewpoint, any

v

study which appears to contradict it, however marginally, should receive considerable attention. Their combined effect, however, has been enough to create serious doubts amongst some academics about the robustness of the efficient market proposition, and many appear to interpret the current state of the debate as one of 'wait-and-see'.

Wait-and-see, however, is not an option available to the investor. The investment strategy appropriate in an efficient market is significantly different from the strategy appropriate within a 'beat-the-market' philosophy. An investor cannot invest without effectively taking a stance on the issue. If wait-and-see, therefore, means 'continuing as before', it amounts in practice to a rejection of market efficiency for the majority of investors, and to an endorsement of their observed behaviour of actively pursuing mispriced securities.

It follows that some attempt is necessary to draw from the evidence a positive framework of practical guidelines, not only for investors, but for investment advisers, corporate managers etc. This book examines the evidence for both sides of the dispute, and attempts to demonstrate that even given the existing degree of conflict in the research findings, it is possible to reach a number of significant conclusions, and to derive some important practical decision-rules for all parties engaged in stock market activities. For the great majority of market participants, it will be argued, *perfect* efficiency is not a necessary condition to justify a substantial rejection of the philosophy associated with the tradition of market inefficiency.

The book is designed for both graduate and undergraduate students of finance, accounting and business studies. It is hoped also that it will be of interest to practitioners—investors, bankers etc. and to anyone else associated directly or indirectly with the securities market.

I owe a number of debts of gratitude in the writing of the book. I am particularly grateful for their comments on the manuscript to Professor William Beaver of Stanford University, Professor Gary Biddle of Chicago University, Professor Bryan Carsberg of the London School of Economics, Professor Richard Morris of Liverpool University, and to my colleagues at Glasgow and Strathclyde Universities. Finally, I would like to acknowledge the support and patience of my wife, Mary, and my daughter, Kerry, both of whom, I think, are finally convinced.

Simon M. Keane
University of Glasgow
September, 1982

1

Introduction

This book is about the stock market. Not about how it operates, or how it is regulated, but about how effective it is in setting prices which reflect the worth of the securities traded in the market. Strictly it is not about any specific stock market. Although most of the empirical evidence reviewed in the text relates directly to the US and UK markets, the general issues and principles involved are relevant to any organised securities market, even if the conclusions reached may have to be tempered to individual conditions.

The market as we know it in practice, its infrastructure, its legends, its reputation, are all firmly founded on the belief that it is not a reliable price-setter, and that it frequently, and sometimes significantly, misinterprets the economic signals it receives. The investment process, therefore, is popularly represented as consisting of the discovery and purchase of securities which are undervalued and of holding these until they cease to be 'good value'. 'Buy when they're low and sell when they're high' is a fundamental if somewhat uninstructive adage of the market. Successful identification of mispriced securities is generally assumed to be possible by personal study of relevant available information, or by seeking out expert advice in the form of investment advisory services, stockbrokers' research departments, or financial press tipsters. Investment intermediaries such as mutual funds, investment trusts etc., compete with one another in an effort to persuade investors that their performance is superior to that of others, and that this superiority is likely to persist in the future. 'Buy-hold-sell' activity, therefore, is an essential charcteristic of the conventional 'beat-the-market' philosophy.

The same philosophy has affected the character of financial reporting which is conventionally perceived as having as one of its principal aims the provision of information that might help the ordinary security holder to formulate buy-sell decisions. The assumption is that, if he is reasonably well-informed and diligent, it is possible for him to arrive at valuations of securities that make more effective use of the information than the market.

The market's reputation as price-setter is derived from two main sources:

(a) the 'official' body of research literature, which by and large conforms as far as possible to the rigours of statistical research methodology and

(b) the experiences, personal impressions and anecdotes that pass from one investor to another and combine to make up the legends of the market. 'Keynes successfully played the market', and 'the market is characterised by the herd instinct', are examples of the second source.

This book is about both sources, the first because, in the end, it is the only valid basis for deciding the issue, and the second because there is reason to believe that the legends etc. of the market are the primary source of many investors' beliefs, and create a barrier to an objective assessment of the alternative source.

The Importance of Efficient Market Theory

But why is the body of literature frequently referred to as the Efficient Market Hypothesis important? Why does it matter whether share prices are substantially 'correct' or not, apart from the fact that if they are, it would suggest that a large section of the investment community is guilty of massive self-deception? The basic reason is a very practical one, that the potential implications of market efficiency are far-reaching for all those connected with the market, and because already the accumulated evidence provides grounds for believing that a significant portion of EMH should now be accepted as the orthodox view.

The creation of wealth depends on the optimal allocation of investment capital, and it is through the securities market that this allocation is most likely to be achieved. If security prices can be relied upon to reflect the economic signals which the market receives, then they can also be looked to in turn to provide useful signals to both suppliers and users of capital, the former for the purposes of constructing their investment portfolios, and the latter for establishing criteria for the efficient disposition of the funds at their disposal. Lack of confidence in the pricing efficiency of the market tends to focus the attention of both investors and raisers of capital on potentially wasteful techniques of exploiting perceived inefficiencies, and away from a more positive recognition of the messages contained in the market's prices.

It is important therefore to know whether the market's pricing mechanism is reliable, because, to the extent that it is, a set of decision-rules significantly different from those which are customarily advocated amongst market participators can be shown to be appropriate. Hence the emphasis in later chapters on the practical implications of market efficiency. It is not possible indeed to give adequate expression to the importance of the efficient market principle until these implications have been fully explored.

The Issues

But the issue is not a simple one. The problem is more than a matter of finding a 'yes' or 'no' answer to the question 'is the market efficient'. There are in fact not one but several issues all of which need to be addressed before the prime issue can satisfactorily be decided. For example:

What precisely does market efficiency mean?

Does its efficiency need to be proved conclusively before it has practical relevance for investors and others?

Is it enough to find a single inefficiency for the market to be validly described as 'inefficient'?

Is it possible for the market to be efficient for one investor and not for another?

Is it possible for the market to be efficient if some investors act irrationally and do not have equal access to, or equal understanding of, available information?

Does the attraction of the stock market depend on its being inefficient?

Is it possible for an efficient market to remain so if all investors come to believe in EMH?

If the market is efficient, how should this affect the behaviour of investors, investment advisers, corporate managers and accountants?

It would be an oversimplification to suggest that opinion on the matter can be divided into those who believe in efficiency and those who do not. The views held by investors doubtless range from total belief in the market's efficiency to total disbelief, with various degrees of scepticism in between. For the sake of discussion, however, it is frequently convenient to speak of two camps. It would be misleading to suggest that the two extreme camps are exclusively composed respectively of academics and practitioners. There are undoubtedly academics who believe the market to be inefficient and act accordingly. There are also likely to be practitioners who by and large are prepared to take security prices as the best estimate of a share's worth. Nonetheless, it is probably fair to state that a very high proportion of those who accept the general substance of EMH are academics and that most of those whose behaviour and professional activities are founded on the premise that the market is inefficient are, by definition, practitioners.

The reason for this can be assumed to be due, partly at any rate, to the fact that the official evidence, by its very nature, has to be collected and evaluated mainly by trained researchers, whilst practitioners tend to form their judgments from their personal experience. It is one of the principal theses of this book that casual personal experience is an unreliable guide and tends more often than not to support the illusion of inefficiency.

And it is this that provides the fundamental reason for the book, the need to bridge the gap between the two camps. The attempt to do so, of course, could be interpreted simply as an effort to provide the practitioner's camp with a clarification of the 'researcher's view,' and in a sense this is correct. The reasons are twofold. First, the researcher's language and techniques are complex and tend to be somewhat obscure to the layman, and are, therefore, more in need of translation than the practitioner's view. Second, the tools of the researcher, as Chapter 2 will seek to demonstrate, are the only valid ones by which the debate can be resolved.

The issue is commonly presented in terms which suggest that what is at stake is whether the market is perfectly efficient, and that, if it cannot be proved to be so, then current investment practices and philosophies can be assumed to be substantially vindicated. This book seeks to demonstrate that the important issue is something quite different—not whether the market is perfectly efficient, but whether the market is efficient enough for it to serve the interests of most investors to behave as if it were perfectly efficient. The critical question, therefore, which the investor has to face is not the indeterminable one 'is the market efficient', but the essentially practical one 'is the market efficient for him'.

Is the Securities Market Likely to be Efficient?

Although much of efficient market theory has potential relevance for markets other than the securities market, not only for those that are closely related such as the foreign exchange market, but for less obvious ones such as the property and antiques markets, the discussion that follows is restricted to the securities market. It needs to be stressed, however, that the verdict on security market efficiency should be reached independently of any perception one might have of the efficiency of these other markets, not least because a number of factors combine to make the securities market more likely than most to be capable of generating prices that fully reflect the worth of the assets being traded. These factors include the homogeneity of the product, its independence from investors' tastes, its location-independence, and the market's extensive informational support.

Homogeneity

Unlike the antiques market, for instance, which is effectively a conglomeration of numerous submarkets, the securities market comprises substantially a single product, the claim to future returns subject to risk. Although the industrial operations that underly securities are diverse and individualistic, the securities themselves provide essentially the same type of product and are therefore highly substitutable. Whatever class of security or type of industry is involved, whatever the location of the enterprise or the currency in which the securities are expressed, all securities are reducible to two important variables—expected return and risk—and this feature provides a degree of comparability within the price structure of the securities market that distinguishes it significantly from most other markets.

Taste-Independence

What makes a particular painting more valuable than another is largely a matter of taste. There is no pricing model that can readily explain the relative difference in value of a Degas and a Dali. But the value of a security is substantially independent of taste. A specific risk-return combination can be assumed normally to have a particular value to investors whatever its mode. Unlike assets which have non-monetary dimensions, the only aspect of a security which might conceivably be vulnerable to investors' preferences is the level of its risk. But it will be shown in the text that one of the more significant conclusions of modern portfolio theory is that the value of individual securities is directly independent of investors' tastes with respect to risk. Certainly, in aggregate, their tastes will affect the value of the market portfolio of all risky assets relative to the value of a riskless asset, but taste should not affect the value of individual securities relative to one another.

Location-Independence

For obvious reasons an undervalued apartment in San Francisco is unlikely to attract much interest from New York residents, and still less from those in London. Even a more transferable commodity such as a Chippendale chair for auction in San Francisco is unlikely to have its price significantly affected by antique collectors in London who can neither see nor touch it. The values of most commodities are therefore, in part at least, dependent on their physical attributes. But the values of intangible assets such as securities are substantially independent of location. The shares of General Motors, if mispriced, are potentially no less of interest to the New Yorker than to the San Franciscan, and may be of equal interest to the Londoner if foreign exchange barriers are absent. Securities are therefore more likely than most commodities to be under constant and intense scrutiny.

Information Support

Perhaps the most outstanding feature of the securities market, and the one that more especially sets it apart from others is the highly organised and elaborate information machinery which services it. It differs from most other markets not simply in the quality and amount of the information supply, but in the rapidity with which the information is disseminated amongst market participants. Information communicators in the securities market have traditionally made the fullest use of current technology to a far greater degree than is found in most other markets, a tradition which presumably owes much to the influence of the three preceding characteristics. Thus, the homogeneity of the product reduces the compass of the informational demand and establishes the focus of relevance on the two variables, risk and expected return. Taste-independence reduces the range of investors' potential information needs. Location-independence provides the necessary motivation for seeking rapid and widespread dissemination.

These characteristics are not enough in themselves to ensure an efficient market, but they do distinguish the securities market from most other markets sufficiently to cause it to come nearer to the economist's concept of the perfectly competitive market. Therefore, although the principles of efficient market theory have wider relevance, it is appropriate in this instance to confine the debate to the market setting where they are most likely to have some validity.

In Chapter 2, the meaning of efficiency is explored, and the reasons developed why the issue can properly be resolved only by rigorous statistical research. Chapter 3 seeks to show why a presumption of efficiency is the most appropriate one to be made by investors etc. until the contrary is proved. Chapters 4 and 5 deal with the official evidence, that is the general body of research literature which investigates the correctness or otherwise of market prices. Chapter 6 investigates the unofficial evidence, the axioms and legends etc. of the market which in practice appear to form the basis of so many investors' beliefs. Then follow three chapters concerned with the implications of market efficiency for various groups directly affected by it.

2

The Efficient Market Hypothesis

The term efficiency, used in its ordinary sense, might suggest that market efficiency relates to the organisational and administrative efficiency of the securities market. The term, however, is used here in a much narrower sense, being concerned specifically with how successful the market is in establishing security prices that reflect the 'worth' of the securities, success being defined in terms of whether the market incorporates all new information in its security prices in a rapid and unbiased manner.

Efficiency, therefore, refers to the two aspects of a price adjustment to new information, the *speed* and *quality* (direction and magnitude) of the adjustment. Sometimes it is suggested that efficient market researchers refer only to the speed aspect. This is quite incorrect.[1] It would be clearly an odd interpretation of efficiency if a doubling in the price of a share were regarded as an efficient reaction to new information, simply because the movement was instantaneous, if the information in fact warranted a substantial reduction in the price. Both aspects of the price reaction are equally important. The main effect of efficiency should be that it precludes most, if not all, investors from being able systematically to outperform the market. Obviously, if the market were deficient in terms of the speed or quality of its reaction, the informed and alert observer would have little difficulty in profiting from the situation.

The Levels of Efficiency

In the literature, a distinction is made between three potential levels of efficiency,[2] each level relating to a specific set of information which is increasingly more comprehensive than the previous one:

(a) *Weak Efficiency*

The market is efficient in the weak sense if share prices fully reflect the information implied by all prior price movements. Price movements in effect are totally independent of previous movements, implying the absence of any price patterns with prophetic significance. As a result, investors are unable to profit from studying charts of past prices. In addition, efficiency at the weak level rules out the validity of 'trading' rules, (such as 'sell a share if it falls by $x\%$ below a certain price') designed to produce above-average returns. Prices would respond only to new information or to new economic events.

(b) *Semi-Strong Efficiency*

The market is efficient in the semi-strong sense if share prices respond instantaneously and without bias to newly published information. Whether or not the users of information might differ amongst themselves about the significance of new data, the implication is that the prices that are actually arrived at in such a market would invariably represent the best interpretation of the information. It would be futile for investors to search for bargain opportunities from an analysis of published data.

(c) *Strong Efficiency*

The market is efficient in the strong sense if share prices fully reflect not only published information but *all* relevant information including data not yet publicly available. If the market were strongly efficient, therefore, even an insider would not be able to profit from his privileged position.

These three levels are not independent of one another. For the market to be efficient in the semi-strong sense it must also be efficient in the weak sense, because if price movements follow a predictable path which the perceptive observer can exploit profitably, the implication is that the price has reacted slowly or capriciously to published information. Likewise, for the market to be efficient in the strong sense, it must also be efficient at the two lower levels, otherwise the price would not capture *all* relevant information.

The conventional view implies that the market is inefficient, possibly in all three senses above. Hence:

The *chartist* seeks to predict future movements by seeking to interpret past patterns on the assumption that 'history tends to repeat itself'.

The *fundamental* analyst studies corporate financial reports and other relevant available information to try to gain an insight into the 'real worth' of shares in the hope of identifying those that the market has mispriced.

The *inside dealer* seeks to acquire information not yet publicly available for the purposes of exploiting it before it is transmitted to the market.

The conventional view, therefore, may be described as the Inefficient Market Hypothesis, since it is obvious that, if it is to be worthwhile for investors to engage in any of the above activities, one must assume that the market is, in fact, inefficient. The implication of efficiency, in its strong sense, is that share prices always reflect their intrinsic worth and can be taken at their face value.

Although the first tests of market efficiency were reported as long ago as 1900,[3] the classification of efficiency into three levels did not emerge until 1959[4] since it was not until the fifties that research in the area systematically developed. Earlier classifications of efficient market literature tended to be dominated by the names of the models which were used to describe share price behaviour and formulated to endow the concept of market efficiency with testable implications.

The most general of these models was the 'fair game' model which expresses efficiency in terms of the opportunities for speculators to earn excess returns. The 'submartingale' and 'random walk' models were two special cases of the fair game model, and are more specifically concerned with the sequence of price changes over time. For example, the submartingale model states that the expected value of tomorrow's share price in an efficient market should be equal to or greater than today's price. This corresponds with the observed fact that shares have a long-run tendency to increase in value. Clearly, prices do fall at times, but if the market is unpredictable, the expectation in a statistical sense is that the next movement will be zero or fractionally upward. The better known random walk model, which has popularly been used at times to denote the whole area of efficient market research, defines market efficiency in terms of lack of dependence between successive price movements, the market being efficient in relation to the information set contained in the past history of prices if share price movements are independent of previous movements. Understanding the precise differences between these models is unnecessary for our purposes. It is sufficient to view them simply as research devices for determining whether observed sequences of share price movements are amenable to exploitation by investors, and therefore as part of the technology of the weak form of efficient market theory.

Which Market?

Some clarification is required about precisely which market is involved in this process. The capital market itself can be viewed as being composed of three distinct markets: (1) the Capital Allocation Market, where funds from savers are distributed amongst productive users of capital; (2) the Financial Securities Market, where the securities owned by the suppliers of capital are traded by them; and (3) the Financial Information Market, where information is transmitted by, amongst others, the productive users of capital to the suppliers.

In a sense, the now standard classification of market efficiency into three levels is somewhat misleading when considered in the context of the above distinction between the securities and information markets. Only the weak and semi-strong levels are concerned with the processing of information, and, therefore, strictly they alone relate to the security market's pricing mechanism. Strong level efficiency is concerned almost exclusively with the production of information, and therefore relates to the efficiency of the information market. If the capital market is found to be inefficient in the strong sense, then it follows that this is a criticism of the information market and of corporate financial reporting practices, rather than of the pricing efficiency of the securities market, since the latter cannot reasonably be faulted for failing to adjust its prices to information that it has not received. For this reason, therefore, the subsequent discussion centres on the semi-strong form as the key level of efficiency in the debate. As for the capital allocation market, the question whether security pricing efficiency is enough to ensure optimal allocation of capital between firms is a separate and more complex issue beyond the scope of this book.

The Assumptions Underlying EMH

There are no significant assumptions upon which the validity of market efficiency depends. It is not a proposition premised on a particular view of the world. It is not conditional upon there being a certain proportion, let alone a majority, of skilled investors. There is no assumption that most or indeed any investors have access to or comprehend all available information, or are in agreement about the significance of the information. The only assumption that EMH can be said to depend upon is one which states that it is *possible*, notwithstanding the existence of naive investors, and despite the activities of speculators and the claims by analysts to possess superior skills, that the market is nonetheless successful in generating prices that instantaneously and correctly capture all new information. And the only assertion that EMH makes is that this possibility is amenable to verification only by rigorous empirical analysis.

This latter assertion, however, is not one that is recognised by many holders of the conventional view, who frequently defend their position with non-empirical arguments. It is necessary, therefore, that the essentially empirical nature of the problem be demonstrated.

Efficiency is Purely an Empirical Issue

Efficient market theory has recently been recognised as essentially a subset of a broader concept in economic theory, the rational expectations hypothesis which has come to play an increasingly significant role in macroeconomic analysis.[5] The rational expectations hypothesis (REH) states that, in a competitive world, economic agents will exploit all available information to take advantage of any perceived profit opportunities. The implication of REH is not that economic agents are omniscient but that they 'do not make systematic mistakes in forecasting the future'[6] and that the drive for profit will tend to eliminate any obvious opportunities for abnormal gain.

Although the significance of REH has been discussed more in the context of other markets such as the labour market, the evidence favouring the security market's efficient use of information has been interpreted as a near perfect illustration of the operation of rational expectations.[7] This is not to say, however, that market efficiency could or should be accepted as a valid proposition simply because it conforms neatly to some such theory. Indeed, it needs to be stressed that although EMH has this close relationship to REH, it appears to have developed as a quite separate phenomenon. The concept of market efficiency did not originate as a theory devised by academics which researchers are now seeking to justify, any more than the notion that inhaling tobacco contributes to lung cancer is purely a theoretical construct. The former derives from a body of conclusions drawn from a mass of empirical tests carried out by researchers since the fifties in the USA, the UK and several other countries. Few, if any, of those researchers would have a vested interest in trying to prove that the market is efficient. On the contrary, if a researcher could uncover a material inefficiency in the market, this could be financially very rewarding for him. In addition, there has now been so much accumulated evidence in favour of efficiency that considerably more attention would follow the discovery of a major inefficiency than any study that merely confirms what has already been repeatedly found in previous studies.

Given the widespread failure to recognise the empirical support for EMH, it is unfortunate that the label 'hypothesis' has been conventionally attached to the underlying evidence. The practice undoubtedly derives from the statistical origins of the concept. When a stastistician carries out an empirical investigation, he must establish an hypothesis which can then be substantiated or refuted by the tests. It is an integral part of the procedure. In this instance, however, the term has by usage been extended to denote the findings from the research in addition to the hypothesis being tested. The danger, regrettably, is that anyone not familiar with the empirical literature might casually deduce that there is no evidence available. Without doubt, fewer people might be persuaded about the injurious effects of smoking if scientists referred to the evidence as the 'tobacco–cancer hypothesis'. In an effort not to perpetuate this confusion, EMH will hereafter be described, wherever the sense allows, as *Market Efficiency*, and the conventional view as *Market Inefficiency*.

The question is, can the efficiency of the market validly be established or refuted by any means other than statistical? The basic characteristic of an efficient market is that it is only luck rather than ingenuity which will allow investors to perform better (or worse) than the market. As we have seen, there is no *a priori* assumption that the market is likely to be efficient, or assumption about the proportion of investors that need to be knowledgeable or rational to make it efficient, or assumption that outperforming the market is anything other than an everyday occurrence. The issue simply is to distinguish between the results of chance and skill.

To illustrate the need for an objective, statistical approach, let it be assumed for the moment that the market is in fact efficient, and that share prices correctly reflect all public information. Imagine also that each of three investors who are totally convinced that the market is efficient is given a different, randomly selected share of equal risk. After a year, the performance of the three shares will almost certainly differ. One investor may possibly have earned a higher return than the market as a whole. What conclusion can be drawn? The investor with the best results would appear rather foolish if he were to claim that the outcome was due in any way to his personal skill. He knew the market to be efficient and he had no part in the selection of the share. There is no reasonable conclusion possible other than that he was fortunate. It follows, therefore, that the existence of investors who have successfully 'beaten the market' can never in itself validly be presented as evidence that the market is inefficient.

Now, assume that the circumstances above are unchanged except for the fact that the three investors were permitted personally to select their own share. At the end of the year, there would now be a strong temptation by the winner to express doubts about the market's efficiency and to attribute his superior results to his personal skill. The other investors would properly point out that the results were perfectly consistent with market efficiency and that, therefore, he had no grounds for suggesting that his 'performance' was due to anything other than chance. The conclusion may be drawn, however, that even if the market were known to be efficient, there would be a tendency by some investors to find the evidence unpalatable, and to disparage it. But the fact remains that even if investors claim to have outperformed the market, and can prove that they have done so, this does not in itself constitute evidence that the market is inefficient.

Finally, assume that the three investors do not know whether the market is efficient, and that they, once again, personally select their respective shares. At the year end, it would now be outwardly more plausible for the winner to attribute his results to superior analysis, and it might seem churlish for the losers to suggest that the results could have been due entirely to good fortune. Once again, however, it is clear that the results may have been due to chance. The conclusion may be drawn, therefore, that if the real world is one where most investors do not believe that the market is efficient, and some of them claim to be able to outperform the market, and at times are observed to do so, this does not in any way affect the reality of the issue as to whether the market is or is not efficient.

How then can the issue be resolved? The winner could attempt to justify the claim that his decision was better than the market's by arguing that he had made a sophisticated analysis of the available information and that, since the market is composed mainly of naive investors, it is not unreasonable to assume that his results were due to skill rather than to luck. The loser could counter this argument by suggesting that perhaps other sophisticated investors had already recognised the implications of the information and caused the share price to react fully at the time the information was published. The subsequent share price movement could have been due to other, unforeseen circumstances. In other words, any disruption of share prices that might be caused by the actions of naive investors may perhaps in practice be neutralised by the instantaneous response of sophisticated investors. The latter, in effect, may be the price-setters.

Now, both of these arguments are reasonable, and in the absence of any firm evidence, one could be excused for taking either side. The fact that most investors appear to have opted for the view that the market is inefficient[8] does not alter the conclusion that this is merely speculative opinion, and that the matter can only be resolved empirically. It should be clear now that the issue is not whether investors can outperform the market. That is easily proved to be true. The issue is whether skilled investors outperform the market by virtue of their *skill* or by *chance*. To establish the former it is essential to demonstrate long-run consistency, and since it is virtually impossible for any individual to distinguish between chance results and systematic skill from casual observation, the conclusions which individuals draw from their personal experience have little relevance or validity. The matter can only be resolved by rigorous statistical testing and analysis.

There are probably few issues which are, in fact, so exclusively statistical in essence as the question of market efficiency, given that the problem is concerned with whether deviations from the average return are systematic or due to chance. For example, reference was made earlier to the problem of recognising the association of tobacco with lung cancer. It is conceivable that microscopic examination might have revealed the presence of inherently carcinogenic substances in tobacco before any statistical field tests were carried out. But no such opportunity for microscopic analysis presents itself with respect to the pricing efficiency of the securities market. Nor is there any intrinsic, philosophical framework which can be used to determine the issue. The only acceptable test is to submit a significant number of investment decisions to controlled statistical analysis over a sufficiently long period to allow for the element of chance.

This dependency on statistical methods has been emphasised here because, despite its obvious validity, it is an unfortunate fact that no single argument is presented more frequently by the traditional sceptic than the observation that 'some investors have beaten the market'. The observation, of course, is statistically insignificant, although the argument employs precisely the same reasoning process as the statistician does, namely observation followed by inference. The difference is that the individual draws his statistical sample from personal experience which, as we have seen, is not only very limited and impressionistic, but because of the natural tendency to be reticent about failures, is apt to be significantly biased. There is, in the end, no valid alternative to a scientifically controlled investigation.

Finally, it is desirable for a moment to anticipate the next chapter in order to note that, despite the fact that the statistical method provides the only valid vehicle for establishing a case in favour of or against market efficiency, even this can never be capable of providing conclusive proof. If for no other reason than that it is impossible to identify every conceivable investment trading rule, the decision about market efficiency must in the last analysis be based on the balance of probabilities in the light of available evidence.

Can Share Prices be 'Correct'?

It is common practice by writers to depict the concept of efficiency in terms of share prices being correct or incorrect. Despite the potential usefulness of the expressions, however, they are sometimes objected to on the grounds that the attribute of correctness implies a level of accuracy and objectivity that cannot be found in a share price. Share prices, it is claimed, reflect no more than a consensus, and because of the lack of any objective benchmark against which correctness can be judged, it must

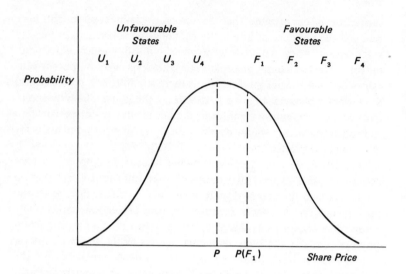

Figure 2.1   *Probability of change in current share price (P) at time t_0 given possible future states of the world at time t_1, favourable (F) or unfavourable (U)*

always remain a matter of individual judgment whether a specific share price is correct or not.

Two issues arise therefore: what does a correct price mean, and is it legitimate to refer to share prices in such terms?

Definition of Correctness

The price of a share is analogous to a bet at a race-track. The price P in Figure 2.1 is correct if the 'odds' it represents at time t_0 are fair compared to those of all other prices, and if they fully reflect the probabilities of all future states of the world that could affect the company. The essence of a correct price is not that it predicts the future, but that it fully captures the uncertainties of the future. If, without any change in circumstances, the price were to move to $P(F_1)$ it would cease to be correct because it would give undue weight to one or more of the possible favourable states of the world. Even if state F_1 should subsequently transpire at time t_1, price $P(F_1)$ at time t_0 would have been incorrect. Like all decisions, the correctness of a price depends not on the final outcome, but on the efficient use of the information at the time of the price decision.

Verification of Correctness

There is no acceptable yardstick for determining correctness at the time a price is observed. Concurrent assessment is purely subjective because it always remains open for an investor to specify and defend a different set of states of the world and a different set of probabilities. It is, however, a subjective assessment about an objective phenomenon, namely whether the odds attached to a bet offer the bettor an expected return that compensates for the risks involved and is consistent with the returns on other similar bets. As such, and unlike the assessment of an intrinsically subjective phenomenon like beauty, it is verifiable. But verification has to be retrospective, although, even then, it can never be very specific about individual prices. It has already been stressed that the goodness of an individual decision cannot be judged simply by its outcome. If state of the world F_1 transpires with respect to the share in Figure 2.1, its occurrence would not refute the correctness of the price P, any more than an unchanged state of the world would confirm it. The analysis must embrace a significant number of pricing decisions because the task is to evaluate the market's choice of odds at time t_0 against the opinions of those who claim at time t_0 that the odds are incorrect, and the only acceptable method is to study a sufficient number of market decisions against a sufficient number of individual opinions to minimise any distortion that might result from the analysis of single decisions. Hence the previous emphasis on the need for a statistical approach.

Therefore, even although accuracy and objectivity are largely elusive properties in the contemporaneous assessment of correctness, they may find acceptable levels in the retrospective verification process. And this indeed underscores the problem encountered by the traditional investor. Although there are undoubted problems in the research technology used for assessing correctness retrospectively, nonetheless, as the level of research sophistication increases, so consequently does the level of accuracy and objectivity attainable in the verification process, highlighting the contrasting fragility of the bargain-hunter's task, and the tendency, as market competition intensifies, for the process of perceiving correctness or incorrectness to become increasingly more exacting.

It is true that if retrospective analysis reveals the presence of a systematic mispricing by the market, such as a tendency for share prices in May to be consistently lower than prices in the Autumn, the investment decision to buy in May could in a sense be said to 'follow' the verification process and to inherit some of the greater level of accuracy and objectivity of the latter. But if the alleged mispricing is non-systematic, that is, a 'special situation', the decision is purely judgmental, and unless the degree of inefficiency is significant, is likely to call for a fairly fine assessment of what is or is not the correct price. The traditional investor's case is inescapably founded on the premise that incorrectness can be identified, if not with accuracy and objectivity, at least with sufficient confidence to make the pursuit of mispriced securities a rational activity.

In summary, there is merit at times in discussing the issue of efficiency in terms of share prices being correct or incorrect. The validity of the term is not diminished by the fact that at the critical stage of making investment decisions, the correctness or otherwise of share prices is essentially a subjective assessment. The object of the efficient market debate is not to determine whether current share prices can be demonstrated to be correct, but whether the evidence relating to past prices is sufficient to warrant the *assumption* that current prices are correct.

Intrinsic Worth

It is now possible to define a closely related concept, the 'worth' of a share. If the market correctly 'sets the odds', the price of a share will represent its worth. The latter, therefore, denotes the best valuation of a share in relation to available information. It does not signify that an investor is assured of any particular given return from the security, only that the price fully reflects all the risks associated with the company's future, and that the expected return (the average of all possible returns) is commensurate with those risks. Nor does a share have a worth in an absolute sense. A share can be truly worth one price today and a totally different price tomorrow if the future outlook changes in the meantime. The new worth does not in any way invalidate the earlier one. At any given point of time, therefore, a security is worth its market price if, after allowing for any differences in risk, the price is consistent with the prices of all other securities.[9]

It is clear from this definition that, despite a common tendency for writers to use the terms interchangeably, worth is distinguishable from value. The latter is an *estimate* of worth. Hence the share price represents the market value and is the market's estimate of worth. It reflects the consensus. It is not necessarily equal to the worth of the share if the market is inefficient. Indeed, it is the essence of the traditionalist's case that market value frequently differs from a share's worth. An individual investor might value a share at $10, whilst the market value or price is $12. Yet the worth of the share may be $11 if the market is inefficient. Like correctness, however, worth is not directly observable and verification is essentially a retrospective process.

The view is sometimes expressed that the price of a share represents its worth, irrespective of whether one agrees with the price or not. But this is to use the term 'worth' synonymously with market value. There is of course no dispute about whether price is equal to market value. The whole issue is whether it is equal to the share's worth.

Adopting the terminology used earlier to describe the different levels of efficiency, it is possible to distinguish two categories of worth:

Semi-strong worth, being the best valuation of a share in relation to the published set of relevant information.

Strong worth, being the best valuation of a share in relation to the total set of relevant information, including information not yet published. This is what is generally referred to as 'intrinsic worth'.

It follows that the securities market is an efficient user of information if listed security prices represent their semi-strong worth and that the information market is an efficient supplier of information if security prices represent their strong worth. It will be argued in Chapter 9 that the ideal goal of corporate disclosure policy is to achieve a state where security prices represent their strong worth.

Conclusion

The efficiency of the securities market relates to the speed and quality of its reaction to information. If the market reacts efficiently to public information, the price of a share will equal its semi-strong worth. If the market reflects all information efficiently, including 'private' information, the price of a share will equal its strong or intrinsic worth. These are not issues, however, that can be determined by the study of individual or even a small number of investment transactions. Market efficiency does not imply that individual shares will consistently earn their expected return, or that the investment performances of investors will always be the same. It does imply, however, that the *central tendency* will be for shares to earn their expected return, and that investors will achieve abnormal returns only by chance. The issue whether the market is efficient in this sense can be solved, therefore, only by the rigorous testing and analysis of large numbers of investment transactions over significant periods of time.

Notes and References

1. See, for example, Beaver, W. (1981) *Financial Reporting: An Accounting Revolution*, Prentice-Hall, Ch. 6.
2. Fama, E. (1970) 'Efficient capital markets: a review of theory and empirical work', *Journal of Finance*, May.
3. Bachelier, L. (1900) *Théorie de la spéculation*, Gauthiers-Villars.
4. Roberts, H.V. (1959) 'Stock market "patterns" and financial analysis: methodological suggestions', *Journal of Finance*, March.
5. Kantor, B. (1979) 'Rational expectations and economic thought', *Journal of Economic Literature*, December.
6. Begg, D. (1982) *The Rational Expectations Revolution in Macroeconomics*, Philip Allan.
7. Kantor, *ibid.* p. 1424.
8. Possible reasons why market inefficiency is the generally accepted view will be discussed in the next chapter.
9. Given investors' personal taxation differences, of course, the worth of a share may not be the same for one investor as for another. Therefore, when shares are said to reflect their worth, it means that, after allowing for personal taxation differences, there is no one share which is better value than another in the same risk class.

3

The Burden of Proof

In subsequent chapters it will be shown that the empirical literature falls into two categories, a high proportion of evidence favouring the conclusion that the market is an efficient information processor, and a small proportion that appears to conflict with this conclusion. This raises the issue, therefore, whether the existence of the latter makes it necessary for investors to suspend judgment about the matter. Does the evidence favouring efficiency need to be unequivocal and overwhelming before assent to it as an economic fact is reasonable? Or is it sufficient to be guided simply by the balance of the existing evidence? Does the market have to be perfectly efficient for EMH to be accepted as valid for practical purposes? Upon whom rests the burden of proof?

Exploitable Inefficiency

There can be little doubt that the received wisdom amongst practitioners is that the market's price-setting mechanism is inefficient. In addition, there appears to be a presumption that the onus of proof rests on the proponents of market efficiency to establish their case convincingly before any doubts about the conventional view should be given serious consideration. There are sound reasons, however, for questioning the validity of this presumption, even before any empirical evidence is considered.

First it is essential to recognise that it is not simply a set of beliefs that is at stake but a set of investment strategies. In Chapter 7 it will be shown that there is a well-defined strategy that follows logically for any investor who believes the market to be efficient, a strategy which involves 'least cost', namely to buy a portfolio as broadly diversified as the market, and to pursue substantially a buy-and-hold policy. In contrast, if the market is assumed to be inefficient, there are incremental costs involved in exploiting the inefficiencies, namely:

(1) the costs of searching for mispriced securities,
(2) transaction costs in switching securities,
(3) the increased risk exposure from inefficient diversification resulting from the pursuit of perceived bargains, and
(4) the opportunity costs of holding cash during non-investment periods.

The combined effect of these costs is to place the burden of proof on those who advocate renouncing the market portfolio in pursuit of inefficiency. In addition, it requires proof of more than the mere existence of an inefficiency. To have operational significance, the inefficiency must be *exploitable*, in the sense that an investor should have a reasonable expectation of profiting from it. And to be exploitable, it should satisfy certain criteria, namely it should be:

(1) *Authentic*—it should be supportable by properly conducted statistical research, after taking into account all relevant factors such as investors' personal tax effects etc.

(2) *Identifiable*—it is not enough to show that some experts or strategies consistently beat the market if these are not identified. Investors are presented continuously with a bewildering number of advisers and investment rules, and if some of these can achieve genuinely superior performances the investor must have a valid basis for distinguishing them from less successful competitors. Without this basis the inefficiencies that they denote may be of no practical consequence to the investor.

(3) *Material*—inefficiencies are not exploitable unless they are sufficient to compensate for the costs and risks of pursuing them.

(4) *Persistent*—it is not sufficient that an inefficiency be shown to have existed in the past, if there are no grounds for believing that it will continue to exist in the future. Hence, even when a material

inefficiency has been identified and authenticated, one must be reasonably satisfied that the market will not learn from the experience.

It may seem unreasonable, having advanced what for many must appear to be a relatively novel and certainly unorthodox hypothesis about the market's pricing mechanism, to proceed immediately to argue that it falls on those who have long believed the opposing view to demonstrate that this hypothesis is false. But it must be stressed that, although the conventional view has enjoyed a long tradition, it too, no less than the efficient market view, is based on a simple belief or hypothesis, namely that some components of the market portfolio are recognisably not worth holding. The question that presents itself is which hypothesis, in the absence of evidence, is the more reasonable basis upon which to found an investment strategy. Since there are some indisputable benefits in holding the market portfolio, and some equally indisputable costs in attempting to compete with it, it is argued that, despite its long tradition, the conventional view deserves no prior claim upon investors' beliefs. It needs to be demonstrated convincingly that the components of the market portfolio which are not worth holding can clearly be identified as such.

Efficient with Respect to Whom?

Even if an exploitable inefficiency is shown to exist, this is not in itself reason enough for the market to be classified as inefficient in a general sense. It is possible for the market to be inefficient to one investor and efficient to another, depending on whether the individual is in a position, directly or indirectly, to take advantage of the inefficiency. To understand why this is so it is useful to draw a distinction between '*judgmental*' and '*rule-of-thumb*' inefficiencies. The former depend for their recognition on the perceptiveness of the investor. For example, if a specific share price at a particular point in time does not fully reflect all publicly available information, this is a judgmental inefficiency, being directly exploitable only by those who have the necessary insight to perceive its existence. In contrast, if tests show, say, that the market consistently overvalues stocks with high Price-Earnings ratios, this is a rule-of-thumb inefficiency available to any investor, whatever his individual information-processing skills might be. As long as he is aware of the decision rule that all high P/E stocks should be avoided, he does not need to be able personally to see through to the substance of the inefficiency.

Now if the market is found to contain one or more exploitable rule-of-thumb inefficiencies, satisfying the four criteria above, then it can truly be said to be inefficient in a general sense, because it would be irrational for any investor to formulate his investment strategy on the basis that the market is efficient with respect to all securities. But if the market's inefficiencies are judgmental and, therefore, perceptible only to those with special skill or insight, it will remain efficient to the remaining body of investors unless the insights of the experts are transmittible to them. However, the simple act of communicating the information, whether by circular, press comment, or whatever, is itself a piece of data which may be instantaneously captured in the market price, in which case the inefficiency is exploitable by no one other than those who directly perceive it. Under these circumstances, the optimal strategy for the majority of investors may be to behave as if the market is efficient even with the knowledge that for others the market is inefficient. To some extent, therefore, market efficiency is a personal issue, where each individual has to decide whether the market is efficient for him, or whether he has enough evidence to count himself amongst the gifted few.

Degrees of Efficiency

How efficient must the market be for EMH to be an acceptable proposition? Before answering this question, it is necessary once again to make a few disctinctions. Firstly, an efficient market is not synonymous with a perfect market. In a perfect market, every investor is rational, has immediate access to all relevant information, and all information is costless. If the market were perfect, it would follow that its pricing mechanism would be efficient. But in reality the market is manifestly imperfect, and, therefore, whether it is efficient remains a matter for investigation.

It is the central thrust of this book that a meaningful verdict on market efficiency can be reached only in terms of how the degree of observed efficiency affects optimal investment behaviour. The market is effectively efficient if it can be shown to serve the interests of investors to behave as if it is efficient. The issue, therefore, is not a simple either/or situation. It is a continuum ranging from perfect efficiency to total inefficiency. For practical purposes, however, it is sufficient to recognise three potential degrees of efficiency in contrast to the simple conventional dichotomy of efficient or inefficient, namely perfect efficiency, near efficiency, and inefficiency. Accordingly, each of the three levels of efficiency —weak, semi-strong and strong—may be characterised by one of these degrees. For example, at the semi-strong level, *PERFECT EFFICIENCY* obtains when prices are so close to their semi-strong worth that not even the most expert information-processor can achieve an excess return for his efforts; *NEAR EFFICIENCY* obtains when prices are sufficiently close to their semi-strong worth to make it futile for all investors other than the expert minority to pursue an active trading strategy, and where the expert earns only enough excess returns to cover transaction costs and reward him for his efforts; *INEFFICIENCY* exists if even the non-expert can perceive mispriced securities or, at least, if he is able to profit from the recommendations of the expert who perceives them. There are, of course, various possible degrees of inefficiency.

Classifying efficiency into three degrees as well as into three levels may appear unnecessarily confusing, but the significance of doing so will become clear as the discussion develops. It is conceivable, for example, that the market could be perfectly efficient at the weak level, near efficient at the semi-strong level, and inefficient at the strong level. For the concept of market efficiency to hold literally, the market would presumably need to be perfectly efficient at all three levels. For market efficiency to hold for most practical purposes, however, it is sufficient for it to be 'near efficient' at the first two levels.

Unless the market is perfectly efficient in the widest sense, it is in fact exceedingly unlikely that its pricing mechanism could be perfectly efficient at the semi-strong level. If prices at all times fully and unequivocally reflected publicly available information, there would be little incentive for market traders to incur the costs of gathering and processing information.[1] Yet if the latter abandoned their activities, the efficiency of the market would presumably break down.

Some might take the view that this need by information-processors to have incentives to perform their function has the effect of placing the burden of proof back into the EMH camp. But the important issue at stake is not whether market efficiency holds in an absolute sense, but whether it holds as a working principle for the great majority of investors. Even if a minority of skilled information-processors are able to earn enough from the market to reward them for their activities, provided their superior insights are not transmittible to the majority, the market can still be classified as near efficient. Hence the burden of proof remains

with those who advocate an active strategy to show that the market cannot
be classified as efficient even in the near sense. It is this issue with which
the subsequent chapters are concerned.

The Illusion of Inefficiency

It is a reasonable assumption that few investors are familiar with the
research literature for or against efficiency. Why then is it, if considerations of self-interest favour a presumption of efficiency, that most investors
appear to act on the assumption that the market is inefficient?

One possible explanation is that investors are subject to an illusion of
inefficiency as a result of a common misconception of how an efficient
market should behave. Such a market has been defined as one where
prices respond instantaneously, and in an unbiased manner, to all new
information, with the result that investors are unable systematically to
make abnormal returns. There are no 'bargain' shares. Incorrectly,
however, efficiency is commonly interpreted to imply that the market
should have the following characteristics:

(1) share price movements will be relatively few in number and
    magnitude,
(2) the rate of return actually earned on any particuar share will
    approximately equal the rate appropriate for the share's risk class,
    and
(3) investors will perform more or less equally, according to the
    degree of risk they are prepared to undertake.

None of these assumptions is valid, their basic error being derived
from the belief that an efficient market is one that should be able to
predict the future. The first assumption fails to recognise that the
market's frequent price movements support rather than call into question the market's efficiency. The market is a barometer, interpreting the
financial implications of the world's political and economic events, and
if the signals received are frequent, then the more sensitive the market is,
the more frequent its share price movements should be in response to
those signals.

The second assumption fails to distinguish between the *ex ante* or
expected return and the *ex post* or actual return. Each share's prospective
returns have already been described in terms of a probability distribution, where the market assigns probabilities to the various possible
future events that can affect the company's fortunes. The expected

return from a share at its current price is the weighted average rate expected from this range of possibilities. If subsequent events turn out to be on either the more favourable side or the more adverse side of this probability distribution, the return actually earned on the share will be more or less than expected. But this is not inconsistent with efficiency. It is even conceivable that, over a given period of time, not a single security in the market will earn its expected rate, although one would assume that in the long term the *average* return actually earned on the market portfolio should approximate the *average* return expected.

Finally, the third assumption fails to recognise that even if no investors can consistently beat the market, large numbers of investors are likely in the short term (perhaps a few years) to perform considerably better or worse than the market average. In the previous chapter, it became clear that if shares are performing differently from one another as a result of chance events, then, provided investors hold portfolios of shares which are not representative of the market as a whole, their performances will differ from one another by chance, at least over the short term. All that efficiency implies is that the different performances cannot be attributed to the skills of the respective investors.

Given these misconceptions, it is not surprising that many investors are subjected to an illusion of market inefficiency. They are exposed daily to numerous events which, from their particular perspective, bear all the hallmarks of inefficiency. They observe particular shares highly prized at one time, falling out of grace another time. They observe the market index fluctuating at times apparently aimlessly. They observe experts claiming to be able to predict price movements, and at times, apparently succeeding. Yet all these observations are quite consistent with market efficiency. If misunderstood, however, they provide a firm base on which the illusion of inefficiency is able to flourish.

In addition, a number of other factors can be identified which further promote the same illusion:

(1)   The Information Gap

Even if the market were perfectly efficient, shares would frequently appear mispriced because individual investors are unlikely ever to be in possession of the same information set as that of the market. In an efficient market all available information will be reflected in the price. The individual will typically have one and possibly several gaps in his own information set, and, therefore, from the perspective of his subset of information, prices will at times appear to be incorrect. Even professional investors will suffer from the same restricted vision, except that they will be able, and at times convincingly, to rationalise the difference between the price they observe and the value they perceive to be correct.

The potentially myopic perspective of the individual relative to that of the group has been vividly illustrated by Beaver[2] in a study of the forecasting skill of a group of football experts. The study found that the consensus forecast was consistently superior to that of any of the individual experts, implying that the informational deficiencies of individuals can to some extent be diversified away. If the same phenomenon operates in the securities market, then it is understandable why an individual analyst might at times be led to believe that the prices he observes are in conflict with available information.

(2) Biased Reporting

Investors tend to report the outcome of their investment transactions in a biased manner. It is the successful recommendations and investment selections that are more frequently reported, which is understandable, given that it is in the interests of those who hold themselves out to possess above average skill to emphasise their successes and to explain away their failures. This bias is evidenced, for example, by the practice of investment fund managers to publicise their results during periods when they happen to be performing better than average, even although several studies support the conclusion that few, if any, of the funds can perform consistently better than chance without access to inside information.

(3) Personal Experience

People also tend to attach more weight to personal experiences than to systematically derived data. The experience of one bad flight is likely to carry more influence on an apprehensive air-traveller's views about the safety of flying than a mass of statistical data. Likewise, if an investor has personally earned, or is acquainted with someone who has earned above average profits, he will be apt to attach undue significance to this event, despite the absence of any rigorous test to determine whether the results were due to anything other than chance. Although the issue of whether the market can be beaten is capable of being resolved only by testing large numbers of transactions, there is no argument presented more frequently by holders of the conventional view than the fact that they 'know someone who has beaten the market'.

(4)   The 'Gambler's Fallacy'

Finally, investors have a tendency to be guilty of what is known as the 'gambler's fallacy', which, in this context, may be described as the belief that what 'goes up must come down'. Thus research indicates that people:

'have difficulty in constructing random sequences and usually judge sequences like HTHTTH to be more random than HHHTTT (it is not). They fall prey to the so-called gambler's fallacy, and even experts have been observed to use the 'law of small numbers' (i.e. they overestimate the reliability of small sample results). After observing a long run of black on a roulette wheel, for example, most people erroneously believe that a red is now due, presumably because the red would make the entire sequence of spins more representative of a random sequence than an additional black. Thus, chance is commonly viewed as a self-correcting process in which deviations in one direction induce deviations in the other so that an equilibrium is restored.'[3]

This phenomenon exhibits itself also amongst investors. A share that has risen consistently for a period is assumed to be 'due for a fall.' The status which the financial press attaches to the previous year's high-low prices supports the existence of this fallacy, implying as it does the tendency for price movements in one direction to induce a counter movement, so that by knowing the relationship of the current price to recent high or low prices, one can better estimate the likely direction of future price movements. This, of course, supports the illusion that the market is predictable and therefore inefficient.

Conclusion

A number of factors can be identified which may explain the readiness of investors generally to presume that the market is inefficient. The demand for rigorous proof of inefficiency is likely to seem pedantic to most investors when the impressions created by the market are so strongly in favour of that presumption. It has been argued in this chapter, however, that if no compelling evidence existed for or against efficiency, then, because of the search costs, transaction expenses and incremental risks associated with the pursuit of potential inefficiencies, the most economically expedient assumption that could be made by the majority of investors is that the market is efficient. It is in their interests to adopt the maximum-diversification, least-cost strategy that is the logical concomitant of efficiency until authentic evidence to justify abandoning such a policy is produced. The fact that there is evidence, and as we shall see, a very considerable body of evidence, supporting the view that the market is a highly efficient information-processor, gives all the more weight to the conclusion that the onus rests with those who argue that the market is characterised by enough inefficiency to validate the conventional active investment philosophy. It is commonly suggested by critics that EMH is 'just a theory'. But, arguably, it is the conventional view that is just a theory, since for many it consists of no more than an act of faith that the active pursuit of bargain opportunities can reasonably be expected to produce enough excess returns to cover the associated costs and risks. Indeed, if EMH is to be criticised for its theoretical content, it is that it lacks theoretical underpinning. What passes for efficient market theory is largely no more than a systematic description of the empirical findings of market researchers. There has been very little theory construction about the processes by which the market's efficiency might come about, and our understanding is very limited in that respect.

The phrase 'just a theory' is perhaps intended to reassure investors that there is no immediate urgency to assent to the notion of efficiency, and to imply that prudence requires conclusive proof before abandoning conventional investment practices. But market efficiency is not the kind of proposition that is amenable to conclusive proof, any more than is market inefficiency. The most that can be shown in favour of efficiency is that no significant inefficiency has been revealed in the past. It is not possible to prove conclusively that no inefficiency will occur in the future. But incontrovertible proof is unnecessary. The burden of proof, to the extent that proof is possible, rests with advocates of the active investment school to establish beyond reasonable doubt the existence of one or more exploitable inefficiencies.

Notes and References

1. Grossman, S.J. and Stiglitz, J.E. (1980) 'On the impossibility of information efficient markets', *American Economic Review*, June.
2. Beaver, W. (1981) *Financial Reporting: An Accounting Revolution*, Prentice-Hall, Ch. 6.
3. Biddle, G. and Joyce, E. (1974) 'Heuristics and biases: their implications for probabilistic inference in auditing', research report submitted to *Research Opportunities in Auditing*, Peat, Marwick, Mitchell & Co.

4

The Evidence I

In the previous two chapters it was emphasised that the market's pricing efficiency is an issue that can be determined only by empirical research. The purpose of this chapter is to provide a brief review of the findings favouring efficiency, since these form the bulk of the empirical literature. The counter-evidence and the problems of researching into market efficiency will be the subject of the following chapter.

The evidence relating to efficiency can be divided into two classes: direct and indirect. Direct evidence concerns the market's reaction to specific items of information. If the item belongs to the set of information relating to past price movements, the test can be described as a direct test of the weak level of efficiency. If the item belongs to the set of information relating to publicly available economic data, then the test is directly one of the semi-strong level of efficiency. The indirect evidence is drawn from a study of the performance of investors as a result of using the information available to them. It does not provide a test of any specific level of efficiency, but a test of all three levels jointly, the significance of which will be discussed in a later section.

Weak-Level Efficiency

The weak-form tests are concerned with the validity of using the past history of prices to predict future prices. It appears to run contrary to

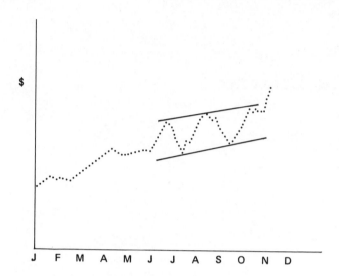

Figure 4.1   *Stock price changes*

intuitive feelings that patterns such as that in Figure 4.1 could be attributable purely to chance. Although it is generally believed that only a minority of professional investors make formal use of the chartist's technology, there are several signs of a fairly wide tacit endorsement of the philosophy underlying chartism. 'The market index has penetrated the 600 barrier', or 'we are currently in a falling market', are everyday observations that reflect the chartist's fundamental perception of market price movements. When an investor states, for instance, that the market 'is falling', he is effectively asserting that, because prices have been observed to fall recently, they have a greater likelihood of continuing to fall than they have of rising. This is no less an expression of chartist principles than the detailed analysis of the peaks and troughs of the pattern in Figure 4.1.

Tests of the weak form of efficiency have their origins in what has come to be known as the *random walk theory*. The latter name derives from a series of market studies carried out by researchers, mainly in the 1950s and 1960s, which indicated that the sequence of share price movements over time, such as that in Figure 4.1, far from forming prophetic patterns, are quite consistent with being a series of cumulative random numbers.

The tests addressed two questions: (a) do prices over time have sufficient serial dependence to allow investors to predict future price movements by studying trends? and (b) can trading strategies based on price movements provide opportunities for abnormal profit?

The first group of tests extends from the early study of Working[1] to the later studies of Kendall,[2] Roberts,[3] Alexander,[4] Granger and Morgenstern,[5] and several others. These have fairly consistently demonstrated that the pattern of share price movements substantially follows a random walk and that price changes are independent of prior movements. The term 'random' is perhaps unfortunate in this context in that it lends itself to being misinterpreted as suggesting that price movements are whimsical or even chaotic. It means, in fact, no such thing. It signifies that prices respond only to new information and, since new information may be randomly good or bad, prices will move in an unpredictable manner. The movements themselves, however, are a perfectly rational response to the information.

This attribute of the market is sometimes described, somewhat misleadingly, in the phrase 'the market has no memory',[6] implying that the market's pricing decisions are not affected by past price levels. The danger of this expression is that it has unfortunate connotations, suggesting a market deficiency. Indeed, we argue later that if a significant inefficiency in the market were disclosed by research, it is likely that the market would indeed remember the experience and, thereafter, adjust its prices to take account of the potential inefficiency.

The second group of tests focuses on the effectiveness of using certain specific trading rules designed to exploit possible systematic patterns in share price movements. One study by Alexander[7] found that abnormal returns could be earned by using certain filter techniques (the name given to a specific type of strategy) but found also that the profits disappeared when transaction costs were taken into account. Similar results were found by Fama[8] and Fama and Blume.[9] The implications of these findings is that although prices do not literally follow a random walk, the degree of non-randomness is insufficient for investors to trade profitably after transaction costs. Some other trading strategies have also been tested, for example, by Latané and Young[10] and Jensen and Bennington,[11] and none was found to be able to outperform a simple passive strategy.

One of the more sophisticated tests of the weak form of efficiency was reported in 1982 by Rosenberg and Rudd.[12] Having observed the lack of serial correlation in the total returns of securities, the authors tested for serial correlation with respect to each of the major components of a security's return. A security's total return is generally recognised to be composed of two major elements, the return that is common to all securities and the return that is specific to the individual security. The study found a positive serial correlation for the common component and a correspondingly negative correlation for the specific component, resulting in an increased predictability of the total returns. Although the findings suggest a violation of the weak form of efficiency, the study ignored the impact of transaction costs, and there was no evidence that the results amounted to an exploitable inefficiency.

The conclusion is generally accepted, therefore, amongst researchers that the market is substantially efficient in the weak sense. Despite the existence of what *appear* to be trends in the historic movement of share prices, and despite the claims by technical analysts that the study of these trend-like patterns can provide insights into future prices, the evidence points firmly to the contrary. It would appear not to be possible to earn sufficient profits to cover costs by using a technical approach to investment selection.

Semi-Strong Efficiency

Most of the subsequent discussion relates to the semi-strong rather than to the strong level of efficiency. The reasons for this are: (a) as indicated in Chapter 2, the strong form is concerned more with the disclosure efficiency of the information market than with the pricing efficiency of the securities market; and (b) both the evidence and intuition suggest that the capital market is not efficient in the strong sense of prices capturing new information before it has been published. There must inevitably at times be a delay between the occurrence of a relevant event (for example, the decision by a managing director to seek a merger) and its transmission to the market and absorption into the market price. Tests do confirm that investors who have access to inside information can earn abnormal profits.[13] It is generally accepted, therefore, that the market is inefficient in the strong sense and it is a reasonable assumption that to some extent it is always likely to be so. The important issue from the point of view of most investors, unable or unwilling to use inside information, is whether the information, once released, is fully and instantaneously captured in the share price. Hence, it is the semi-strong level which is the critical test of pricing efficiency and which in practice gives rise to most of the controversy.

The Direct Evidence

Semi-strong efficiency is concerned with two aspects of the market's reaction to new information, the speed and the correctness of the adjustment. Reaction must not only be rapid, it must be in the right direction and of the right magnitude. Speed is usually, though not always, relatively easy to measure. It is the other aspects that present the problems. An adjustment for risk needs to be incorporated into the tests, so that the returns from securities of different risks can be compared on an equal basis, and, ideally, some yardstick is needed for measuring the size of a price adjustment that ought to be associated with a specific information signal. Some of these problems will be discussed in the next chapter.

Earnings Announcements

The direct approach to testing for semi-strong efficiency is to study the market's reaction to specific types of information and events. Of the many possible items which the market could be expected to react to, the most obvious is perhaps a company's annual earnings' announcement. One of the leading research studies in this respect is that of Ball and Brown[14] who investigated the impact on the market of the earnings announcements of 261 US firms during the period 1957–65.

Their primary object was in fact to evaluate the usefulness of accounting earnings in establishing market prices, rather than directly to test the efficiency of the market. That is, the authors proceeded on the assumption that the market is efficient and set out to discover whether corporate earnings statements appear to be used by the market. But the same study can be examined from a different perspective to gain an insight into the market's efficiency. Thus, if it assumed that accounting earnings are likely to play a material role in setting prices, the results of the research can be studied with respect to the efficiency of the market's response to the announcements.

The procedure adopted was as follows:

(a) A calculation was made of the direction in which the earnings of each company changed compared to the previous year's earnings, after adjusting for any overall directional change in the earnings of companies generally.

(b) The sample was then divided into two groups according to whether the change of the earnings was positive or negative.

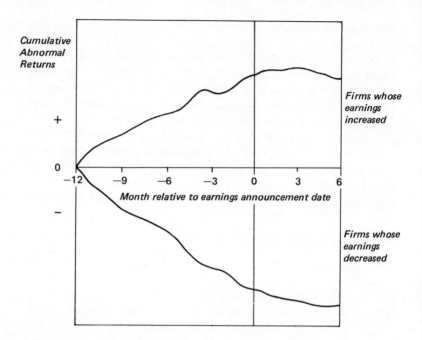

Figure 4.2   *Monthly stock returns and changes in annual earnings*
Source: Ball and Brown (1968) *Journal of Accounting Research*

(c) Finally, the securities of the two groups were tested for any abnormal returns before and after the announcement date compared to securities generally. These abnormal returns could, of course, be positive or negative.

The results are depicted in Figure 4.2, which shows the accumulated abnormal returns of the two groups during the twelve-month period prior to, and the six-month period following the announcement date. They indicate that:

(1) throughout the preceding 12 months, the prices of the shares moved progressively in the same direction as that of the subsequent change of earnings;

(2) as much as 85–90% of the price movement was completed by the
     announcement date, indicating that the market was a good fore-
     caster of earnings, or at least that it had made effective use of other
     sources of information.

The tests, therefore, showed that, whilst earnings data appear to be
relevant for pricing decisions, it would not have been possible for investors
to trade profitably on the basis of the earnings announcement, because
the information was substantially already reflected in the share price.
The fact that the market had largely anticipated the earnings announcement is suggestive but, of course, not conclusive proof that the market's
response was efficient. Presumably, during the prior twelve months, the
market progressively revised its estimates of future earnings in response
to alternative sources of information. Therefore, ideally one would need
to identify those sources in order to determine whether the market's
revisions were timely enough to be classified as efficient.

In addition, the Ball and Brown test was concerned only with the direction of the price movements relative to the direction of the earnings
changes, not with the magnitudes of the respective movements and
changes. But, clearly, if an unexpected change in earnings is of significance to the value of a share, one would expect price movements to be
sensitive to the amount of the change as well as to its direction. A recent
study by Beaver, Clarke and Wright[15] has taken up this point, and intro-
duced specific adjustments to the testing procedures for this purpose.
The results indicate that the market's price changes are in fact quite
sensitive to the magnitude of the change in earnings.

The Market's Forecasting Power

It was noted in the previous study that the fact that the market appears to
react instantaneously to earnings announcements, or even to anticipate
them, does not necessarily rule out the possibility that some investors
might be able to beat-the-market by making superior prior estimates of
earnings changes before the market does. One recent study, however, has
provided some useful insight into the market's capacity to make earnings
forecasts well in advance of publication, and even in advance of the earnings period.[16] A number of earlier studies had attempted to discover the
most successful technique for forecasting a company's earnings a year
ahead. It was found that neither a skilled analyst nor corporate management could on average make forecasts that matched a simple random

walk prediction. That is, the best estimate of next year's profits was found to be this year's profit (subject to a slight adjustment for general drift).

These findings, however, were curiously at odds with the fact that, at any given point in time, the market's price/earnings ratios for shares in the same risk class can vary markedly. The implication of a share with a higher-than-average P/E ratio is that a correspondingly higher-than-average growth in earnings is expected. It is clear, therefore, that the market's predictions of earnings are more positively differential than those of the simple random walk model. The question, therefore, is how does the market's predictive power, as implied by its P/E structure, compare with that of alternative and previously tested techniques. If an efficient market signifies that prices reflect the best estimate of the future, one would expect P/E signals to indicate the most likely changes in future earnings. This in fact was the finding of the Beaver, Lambert and Morse study. A comparison of reported earnings of one year with the next for a sample of companies indicated that the information implicit in the P/E ratio provided the best available predictive tool, thus confirming the market's forecasting power.

Other Items of Information

One of the problems associated with testing the impact of earnings statements on market prices is that it is never possible to be certain when publication effectively takes place. Since the market may be able to form a good estimate of the earnings from recent published announcements of similar companies, this may remove any significant surprise element from its own announcement. Many researchers, therefore, prefer to focus on the impact of cleaner, less predictable events. For example, a pioneer study by Fama *et al.*[17] investigated the market's response to share splits, the rationale being that, although a split in itself may have no economic significance, it may be a signal of management's confidence in the future, and may, therefore, be associated with the occurrence of other more fundamental economic phenomena. To the extent that a split does act as a forerunner of some favourable event, the market should be observed to adjust its prices to reflect this prospect. The results of the study did in fact reveal a tendency for dividends to rise more than average amongst companies that had recently engaged in stock splits. It was also found that market prices adjust to reflect these potentially favourable signals, and that the adjustment appears to be sufficiently complete around the announcement date to prevent investors from profitably trading on the strength of the information.

Another study of semi-strong efficiency by Dann, Mayers and Raab[18] exemplifies the speed of the market's reaction. The research was concerned with the effect on prices of large block trading, the assumption being that a block trade might have informational content for the market if it indicated that the seller or purchaser of the securities had special information. It was found that block transactions did have an effect on prices, but in order to earn a return sufficient to cover transaction costs, investors would have had to react within five minutes of the event. Even if trading costs were zero, it would not have been possible to profit from knowledge of the block trade the day after the event.

A similar result was found more recently[19] in a study of 194 US companies involved in mergers during 1975–8. The market reaction to the announcement of an intended merger was found to be virtually complete within the same day, any delay until the following day being attributable to the fact that some of the announcements were made after the market had closed.

A number of research studies have concentrated on the market's ability to 'see through' changes made by companies in their accounting procedures, for example, changes in depreciation methods,[20] accounting for mergers,[21] inventory valuation techniques,[22] and research and development costs.[23] Apart from a few minor discrepancies, these studies show that the market is not fooled by changes in reported earnings if they are not associated with corresponding changes in the underlying economic conditions.

Other items of information that have been tested for market efficiency, with similar findings, include dividend announcements,[24] changes in the Federal Reserve discount rate,[25] secondary market issues,[26] publication of the Consumer Price Index[27] and money supply statistics.[28]

Clearly, then, the direct approach offers some fruitful insight into the market's response to information, but the task of isolating the extent to which a price movement can be attributed to a specific item or group of items always presents a problem. The amount of direct research has therefore been, and is likely to remain, relatively restricted. Without the support of the indirect approach, the direct evidence is probably insufficient to convince investors of the market's efficiency.

Before proceeding to the indirect evidence, it is perhaps worth noting that chartists sometimes claim that the basis of their case is that prices fully reflect fundamental data and that future price movements, therefore, can only be predicted from studying the pattern of past prices. The implication is that the market may be efficient in the semi-strong sense but inefficient in the weak sense. However, this is not possible. If a price moves significantly in the interval between the release of one item of information and that of another, whether it follows a pattern or not, it cannot at each one of the various levels be equal to the semi-strong worth of the share. A price change without a change in the underlying economic conditions must represent a departure from the semi-strong worth. Hence the market cannot be efficient in the semi-strong sense if it is inefficient in the weak sense.

The Indirect Evidence

The direct approach is concerned with testing the market's *use* of information, that is its reaction to specific items of information at the time of their release. The indirect approach is concerned with the *user* of information, and how he performs over time against some yardstick such as the market average. The direct evidence alone is unlikely ever to be sufficient to provide a decisive case for the market's efficiency. Even if it were possible to test the market's response to every individual item of information that could conceivably make up the public information set, it would always be possible for the protagonist of market inefficiency to argue that it is the insights which the expert acquires as a result of combining several items and sources of information that give him his superior investing power. This power will not necessarily be revealed by examining the market's reaction to the information items individually.

One obvious method of testing this claim is to compare the performance of professionally managed funds against a simple, passive strategy of buy-and-hold-the-market. For this purpose it is not necessary to specify the kind of information or the investment techniques being used by management, because one can assume that if enough funds are tested, all the principal recognised strategies and information sources are being utilised by some managers in some funds. If the market is inefficient in reacting to publicly available information, one could reasonably expect some, if not most, professionally managed funds on average 'to do better than the market'. If the market is efficient, the performance of funds could at best be expected to match the market, and at worst to fall short of it by the amount of management's expenses.

The evaluation of expert performance is in fact a joint test of all three levels of efficiency. If the expert investor is shown consistently to perform better than chance, it may be because he successfully uses chartist or fundamentalist techniques, or because he has access to inside information, or perhaps a combination of all three. Therefore, although the study of expert performance is potentially useful for revealing the existence of inefficiency, it has limited scope for identifying the level at which the inefficiency operates. However, if the evidence indicates that experts are unable to outperform the market, the implication is that the market is efficient at least at the weak and semi-strong levels, since it is reasonable to assume that within the professional investment community some use is made of all principal chartist and fundamentalist strategies. Because there is no certainty that analysts have access to inside information, or that, if they do, they exploit it actively, the implications for strong level efficiency are less clear.

One of the most celebrated tests of this kind is a study by Jensen[29] who examined the performance of 115 mutual funds over the period 1945–64. He found that the funds on average were unable to outperform a passive strategy and that no individual fund was able to perform better than could be expected from random chance. After management expenses were taken into account, most of the funds underperformed a purely passive strategy.

Other studies in the US with similar findings include those of Sharpe,[30] Williamson,[31] Treynor,[32] and Friend, Blume and Crockett.[33] In the UK comparable results were found by Firth,[34] Ward and Saunders[35] and Cranshaw.[36] A recent study by Mains[37] indicated a slightly better result for funds, in that 80% of his sample were able to earn sufficient excess returns to earn back their operating expenses.

A further study by Firth[38] of leading UK financial press tipsters indicated that, to the extent that the press comments contained new information, the prices adjusted instantaneously, with the result that the disciples of the tipsters were unable to benefit from the advice. The implication is, of course, that the tipsters themselves could have benefited. But this, indeed, merely highlights the problem of transmitting investment advice. Even if a specific tipster is known to provide a new source of information, the market apparently responds rapidly enough to prevent other investors from sharing the benefits.

These findings, clearly, have very serious implications for the role of actively managed funds. They do not necessarily imply that investors should avoid investing in them, since funds provide an important diversification vehicle not otherwise available to those with limited amounts of capital. The results, however, do imply that managers, despite their frequent claims to the contrary, are unable consistently to identify under-valued securities. Indeed, a casual survey of the investment literature indicates that proponents of the conventional view tend to interpret this evidence against professional managers as potentially more damaging to their case than the direct evidence for efficiency, and it is against the former that they have largely focused their attacks. A number of arguments have variously been presented in an attempt to discredit the significance of the results. Some of these will now be examined. Given that the next two chapters are devoted to the counter-arguments, it might seem inappropriate at this stage to review arguments levelled against the indirect evidence. But since the arguments involved specifically attack the validity of using the indirect approach as a matter of principle, it is important to consider them now in order to demonstrate clearly that performance-evaluation studies do have a valid role in the debate.

(1) *The poor performance of experts may be due to the market's failure to adjust its (incorrect) prices to accord with the (correct) evaluations of the experts.*

'If the market is as capricious as (the sceptic) suspects, there is little reward to be had from recognising the intrinsic worth of shares, since he cannot rely on the market recognising it within a reasonable time scale. Thus, even if he perceives correctly the intrinsic worth of shares, an investment policy which acts upon this perception will be assured of success only if he is prepared to hold his portfolio indefinitely.'[39]

The implication of this argument is that not only is the market inefficient but that it is exceedingly so. Most researchers, for example, would normally take the view that if share prices do not fully reflect new information within a day or two of publication, the market must be judged inefficient. To argue, however, that the market may consistently fail to react correctly to new information, even long after the correct interpretation has been fully vindicated by subsequent events, is to predicate a very high degree of inefficiency indeed. But even if this extraordinary degree of inefficiency did exist, such that prices obstinately refuse to adjust to the level estimated by the expert, it would still be valid to expect the latter to perform better than average.

For example, if new information about a particular company were interpreted to signify a future stream of dividends of $10 *per annum* in the expert's (correct) estimation, and of $8 *per annum* in the market's (incorrect) estimation, then assuming a 10% capitalisation rate, the market would initially attach a price of $80 to the shares. If the expert made his purchase at this 'bargain' price, then, in broad terms, one of two outcomes could result:

   (a) the share price might subsequently move up to equal the expert's valuation—that is, to $100, producing for him an immediate excess return of 25%;

   (b) the share price might never adjust at any time to the expert's valuation, even though the dividend stream predicted by him is subsequently achieved. This is the extreme inefficiency predicated above. Even in these circumstances, however, the expert will achieve a $12\frac{1}{2}$% return ($10 per $80 share) throughout his holding period as against a 10% normal rate of return.

Therefore, even if the market were as inefficient as the above argument implies, the expert should still be able to achieve superior returns. True, his performance would be less notable the slower the market price adjusts to his valuation. But even if it never adjusts, he should be able to earn abnormally high dividend streams.

(2) *The superior skills of individual managers will not be observed in fund performance.*

'The fruits of fundamental analysis and research . . . will not be discernible in the performance of investors aggregated to comprise major market segments such as mutual funds. Instead, they will remain as individual as the efforts needed to bring them about.'[40]

The implication here is that an individual analyst may be successful in identifying undervalued securities for the fund, but when the effects of his efforts are aggregated with those of his colleagues the benefits of his superior analysis are lost. This suggests either that the benefits are insignificant, or that his colleagues consistently show proportionately lower than average returns such as to cancel out the benefits. If the latter is the case, one would expect management to dismiss the unsuccessful analysts. If the unsuccessful are not distinguishable from the successful, then one must conclude that the allegedly superior skills of the latter are relatively insignificant, or purely hypothetical. Finally, even if the possibility is conceded that talented individuals do exist whose skills are hidden in the aggregate results of funds, this does not constitute an exploitable inefficiency as defined in Chapter 3, since identifiability is a prerequisite of exploitability.

(3) *Rapid changes amongst fund managers make assessment of their performance ineffective.*

> 'In a world in which recognition for success comes rapidly, portfolio managers rapidly reach their levels of incompetence and tend to remain there for some time ... [The competent managers] will move through the successful portfolios of their careers so quickly that their existence will not really be visible to the tests of academics.'[41]

This has been described by one writer as the 'inefficient fund management hypothesis'.[42] It is interesting that market efficiency writers should argue that professional analysts are collectively so skilled in their reaction to new information that they help make the market efficient, when supporters of the conventional view should defend their stance with the argument that managers are too inefficient in general to perform better than chance. Even if it were true that managers were generally prematurely promoted, one would still expect the benefit of their 'successful' analysis in the early stages of their careers to manifest itself in the results of the fund, unless success is measured in terms other than the achievement of above-average returns.

Another writer[43] has gone so far as to argue that the bad performance of professional managers proves that the market is inefficient on the grounds that, if the market were efficient, they should on average perform no worse than the market. But this ignores the fact that the inferior results can be explained substantially by the combined effect of management's salaries, the costs of frequent transactions and the tendency for management to hold a proportion of their capital in liquid form. Although a few studies reveal fund performances that are below expectations for market efficiency, there is no evidence that the shortfall is enough to suggest a systematic tendency for managers to select portfolios with below-average performance.

(4) *The performance of managers may be due to the fact that they all substantially hold the same portfolio.*

> 'Is there not a basic herd instinct at work in the market which causes investors to follow lots of other investors so that they all finish in the middle of the index, not because of efficient pricing mechanisms but because they all hold essentially the same portfolio?'[44]

If it were correct that every fund is effectively a microcosm of the market portfolio, then the performance of each would not only be substantially identical to that of the market, but substantially identical to one another.

But it is a readily observable fact that neither of these positions holds. The evidence indicates not that the funds perform exactly in the same way as the market, but that *on average* over time they perform no better. It is the usual practice each year for a performance league to be drawn up by the financial press where the differences in returns earned by the funds during the year are reported and frequently found to be substantial. This confirms that not all or even most of them hold the market, or hold portfolios identical to one another. Given their differences in composition, there must inevitably be short-term differences in performance. The significance of the empirical evidence is that these short-term differences tend to level out in the long term, implying that managers are unable systematically to select portfolios which earn consistently superior returns after adjusting for risk. This can only be attributed to the fact that the market prices its securities consistently rather than that everyone 'holds essentially the same portfolio'.

(5) *Current research methods are insufficiently refined to identify superior performances.*

'Current statistical techniques cannot detect good or bad performances at levels fund managers can realistically be expected to achieve. Given enough time, genuine outperformers should produce results significantly superior to those of random performers. But the time required undoubtedly exceeds the lifetime of the managers being measured.'[45]

Researchers generally acknowledge that, despite the high degree of sophistication in their current statistical methodology, there is undoubtedly scope for improvement. This issue will be discussed in the next chapter. However, until the effects of using more refined techniques are known, it is not possible to state whether the results will help identify genuinely superior performances, or merely confirm the existing findings. The same author estimates that, even with a better methodology, probably only 20% of managed funds can be expected to outperform a passive portfolio.[46] If only one in five funds, at the most, can be expected to achieve a superior performance, but current statistical techniques are insufficiently refined to detect their superiority, the implication is that it is not only exceedingly difficult systematically to beat the market, but the degree to which it might be beaten is likely to be relatively insignificant.

Nearly all the above arguments against the indirect evidence share a common theme. They speculate about the *possibility* that there might be hidden market inefficiencies in the form of specially gifted managers whom we do not know about. But such a possibility must always exist. It has already been stressed that market efficiency is not amenable to conclusive proof. The important issue is that the mere possibility of their existence is insufficient reason for investors to abandon the principle of a least-cost investment strategy. The onus is on managers to prove that they can outperform the market consistently and to a material extent, and the absence of proof must be interpreted as indirect testimony of the market's pricing efficiency. The allegation that there are inefficiencies unrevealed by research has no operational significance, since their existence can only be established by research.

The Efficiency of Other Securities Markets

The bulk of the evidence relating to stock price behaviour is concerned with the New York and London Stock Exchanges, and the evidence relating to smaller and less developed stock markets is considerably thinner. The extent of the research, however, has increased in recent years, although most of the studies have focused on the more readily testable weak form of efficiency, that is on the randomness of share price movements. For example, tests have been carried out by Solnik[47] into the French, Italian, German, Dutch, Belgian, Swiss and Swedish markets, and it was found that, although the degree of randomness was not as evident as in the US markets, the deviations were insufficient to generate profits after transaction costs in excess of a randomly selected portfolio. Similar findings were obtained by Niarchos[48] in a study of the Greek market, and by Praetz[49] in relation to the Australian market. However, a very high degree of efficiency was found for the Japanese market.[50]

Indications of more significant levels of inefficiency have been found for smaller markets such as those of Singapore, South Africa and Nigeria, the problems arising often by virtue of the size of the markets, the thinness of the trading, and the quality of information disclosure. It is not clear, however, that any significant, exploitable inefficiency has ever been disclosed by researchers.

The evidence relating to the smaller markets is, therefore, somewhat inconclusive in terms of the weak level of efficiency, and exceedingly sparse for semi-strong efficiency. It should be noted, however, that the North American, European and Japanese markets together amount to more than 90% of the world's equity capitalisation.[51] If these markets are substantially efficient, and if capital is allowed to flow across countries, it would be surprising if any inefficiency revealed by research in the smaller markets could survive long enough to give investors elsewhere abnormal profit opportunities.

Conclusion

Considerable evidence, both direct and indirect, supports the conclusion that the market responds efficiently to new information, and that no significant opportunity exists for investors without access to privileged information to outperform the market. But, if the evidence were entirely clear-cut, then presumably market efficiency would by now have become the accepted orthodoxy. It has already been emphasised that the casual empiricism of personal experience tends to militate against belief in efficiency, and that any investor who has not had the opportunity to study the research literature is unlikely to question the conventional view seriously. But even the research literature is not without its problems, and it is with some of these that the next chapter is concerned. It is desirable, therefore, to defer the overall assessment of the evidence until such problems have been reviewed.

Notes and References

1. Working, H. (1934) 'A random difference series for use in the analysis of time series', *Journal of the American Statistical Association*, March. Earlier insights however, had been provided by Bachelier, in 'A study of commodity prices', in 1900.
2. Kendall, R. (1953) 'The analysis of economic time series, part I: prices', *Journal of the Royal Statistical Society*, Vol. 96, Part I.
3. Roberts, H. (1959) 'Stock market "patterns" and financial analysis: methodological suggestions', *Journal of Finance*, March.
4. Alexander, S. (1961) 'Price movements in speculative markets: trends or random walks', *Industrial Management Review*, May, pp. 7–26.
5. Granger, C. and Morgenstern, O. (1963) 'Special analysis of New York Stock Market prices', *Kyklos*, pp. 1–27.
6. Fama, E. (1965) 'Random walks in stock market prices', *Financial Analysts Journal*, September/October, p. 56.
7. Alexander, S. *op. cit.*
8. Fama, E. (1965) 'The behaviour of stock market prices', *Journal of Business*, January.
9. Fama, E. and Blume, M. (1966) 'Filter rules and stock market trading', *Journal of Business, Security Prices: A Supplement*, January. Similar findings were obtained in the UK by Dryden, M. (1970) 'Filter tests of UK share prices', *Applied Economics*, January.

10. Latané, H. and Young, W. (1969) 'Tests of portfolio building rules', *Journal of Finance*, September.
11. Jensen, M. and Bennington, G. (1970) 'Random walks and technical theories: some additional evidence', *Journal of Finance*, May.
12. Rosenberg, B. and Rudd, A. (1982) 'Factor related and specific returns of common stocks: serial correlation and market efficiency', *Journal of Finance*, May.
13. For example, see Collins, D. (1975) 'SEC product-line reporting and market efficiency', *Journal of Financial Economics*, June; Lorie, J. and Nierderhoffer, V. (1968) 'Predictive and statistical properties of insider trading', *Journal of Law and Economics*, April; Jaffe, J. (1974) 'Special information and insider trading', *Journal of Business*, July; and Finnerty, J. (1976) 'Insiders and market efficiency', *Journal of Finance*, September.
14. Ball, R. and Brown, P. (1968) 'An empirical evaluation of accounting income numbers', *Journal of Accounting Research*, Autumn.
15. Beaver, W., Clarke, R. and Wright, W. (1979) 'The association between unsystematic security returns and the magnitude of the earnings forecast error', *Journal of Accounting Research*, Autumn.
16. Beaver, W., Lambert, R. and Morse, D. (1980) 'The information content of security prices', *Journal of Accounting and Economics*, March.
17. Fama, E., Fisher, L., Jensen, M. and Roll, R. (1969) 'The adjustment of stock prices to new information', *International Economic Review*, February.
18. Dann, L., Mayers, D. and Raab, R. (1977) 'Trading rules, large blocks and the speed of adjustment', *Journal of Financial Economics*, January.
19. Keown, A. and Pinkerton, J. (1981) 'Merger announcements and insider trading activity', *Journal of Finance*, September.
20. See, for example, Archibald, T. (1972) 'Stock market reaction to the depreciation switch-back', *Accountancy Review*, January.
21. See Hong, H., Kaplan, R.S. and Mandelker, G. (1978) 'Pooling vs purchase: the effects of accounting for mergers on stock prices', *Accounting Review*, January.
22. See Sunder, S. (1973) 'Relationships between accounting changes and stock prices: problems of measurement and some empirical evidence', *Empirical Research in Accounting: Selected Studies*.
23. Dukes, R. (1976) 'An investigation of the effects of expensing research and development costs on security prices', *Proceedings of the Conference on Topical Research in Accounting*, New York University.
24. See Pettit, R. (1972) 'Dividend announcements, security performances and capital market efficiency', *Journal of Finance*, December.
25. Waud, R. (1970) 'Public interpretation of Federal Reserve discount rate changes: evidence on the announcement effect', *Econometrica*, March.
26. Scholes, M. (1972) 'The market for securities: substitution versus price pressure and the effects of information on share prices', *Journal of Business*, April.
27. Schwerk, G. (1981) 'The adjustment of stock prices to information about inflation', *Journal of Finance*, March.
28. Rogalski, R. and Vinso, J.D. (1977) 'Stock returns, money supply and the direction of causality', *Journal of Finance*, September.

29. Jensen, M. (1968) 'The performance of mutual funds in the period 1945–64', *Journal of Finance*, May.
30. Sharpe, W. (1966) 'Mutual fund performance', *Journal of Business*, January.
31. Williamson, J. (1972) 'Measuring mutual fund performance', *Financial Analysts Journal*, November/December.
32. Treynor, J. (1965) 'How to rate management of investment funds', *Harvard Business Review*, January.
33. Friend, I., Blume, M. and Crockett, J. (1970) *Mutual Funds and other Institutional Investors, A New Perspective*, McGraw-Hill.
34. Firth, M.A. (1977) 'The investment performance of unit trusts in the period 1965–75, *Journal of Money, Credit and Banking*, Vol. 9.
35. Ward, C. and Saunders, A. (1976) 'UK unit trust performance 1964–74', *Journal of Business Finance and Accounting*, Winter.
36. Cranshaw, T.E. (1977) 'The evaluation of investment performance', *Journal of Business*, October.
37. Mains, N.E. (1977) 'Risk, the pricing of capital assets, and the evaluation of investment portfolios: comment', *Journal of Business*, July.
38. Firth, M.A. (1972) 'The performance of share recommendations made by investment analysts and the effects on market efficiency', *Journal of Business Finance*, Summer.
39. See Whittington, G. (1979) 'Beware efficient markets theory', *Accountants Magazine*, August.
40. Bernstein, L.A. (1978) *Financial Statement Analysis*, Irwin, p. 54.
41. Grubel, H. (1979) 'The Peter principle and the efficient market hypothesis', *Financial Analysts Journal*, November/December, p. 72.
42. Glass, R. (1980) letter in *Financial Analysts Journal*, September/October, p. 12.
43. Dreman, D. (1978) 'Don't go with the pros', *Barron's*, May.
44. Brown, E. (1981) book review in *Accountants Magazine*, January, p. 23.
45. Murphy, J.M. (1980) 'Why no one can tell who's winning', *Financial Analysts Journal*, May/June.
46. Murphy, J.M. (1979) 'Second thoughts about the "efficient market"', *Fortune*, February.
47. Solnik, B.H. (1973) 'Note on the validity of the random walk for European stock prices', *Journal of Finance*, December.
48. Niarchos, N.A. (1972) '*The Stock Market in Greece: a statistical analysis*', Athens Stock Exchange.
49. Praetz, P.D. (1969) 'Australian share prices and the random walk hypothesis', *Australian Journal of Statistics* 11.
50. Ang, J.S. and Pohlman, R.A. (1978) 'A note on the price behaviour of Far Eastern stocks', *Journal of International Business Studies*, Spring/Summer.
51. See *Capital International Perspective* (1979) March.

5

The Evidence II (Some Problems)

The purpose of this chapter is to review the arguments directed against market efficiency. Given its length, and the fact that the following chapter is also substantially concerned with counter-arguments, it may seem that disproportionate weight is being attached to reviewing the counter-evidence by comparison with chapter 4's coverage of the evidence favouring efficiency. But it must be recalled that the crucial issue in the debate is not whether the market can be shown to be efficient but whether it can be shown to contain exploitable inefficiencies. All evidence favouring efficiency is of limited consequence if specific inefficiencies can readily be shown to exist. Indeed it would be logically more consistent with the principle that the burden of proof rests with the traditionalist to present the arguments favouring inefficiency first and to offer the EMH evidence as the counter-evidence. The order of presentation selected here is therefore more in deference to considerations of chronology than to those of logic. Prior to the emergence of the EMH literature, no systematic body of evidence had been developed to validate the traditionalist's assumption of inefficiency, other than the intuitive and anecdotal evidence outlined in Chapter 3. It is only in recent years that any significant attempt has been made to counter the general findings of the researcher on his own terms. The case for inefficiency, therefore, remains substantially based on a compilation of the anomalies contained in a few, relatively recent studies and on a critique of the findings and methodology of the evidence favouring efficiency.

The first section of the chapter consists of three case studies which illustrate the difficulties inherent in establishing the existence of a valid inefficiency. The next section considers the significance of the anomalous evidence, followed by a review of the controversy surrounding market efficiency testing procedures. Finally, some criticisms levelled against EMH proponents for the manner in which they present their case are examined.

Three Case Studies

The following cases are presented for the purpose of illustrating the problems encountered by the researcher in determining whether an apparent inefficiency is operationally significant, operational significance being defined in terms of the four criteria identified in Chapter 3: (a) authenticity, (b) identifiability, (c) materiality, and (d) persistence.

(1) *The Impact of Quarterly Earnings Announcements*

One of a group of research findings indicating an apparent inefficiency is a study suggesting that abnormal returns might have been obtained from the analysis of public announcements of quarterly earnings.[1] The period studied covered the six years between 1962 and 1968. It was found that above normal returns could have been earned between 1962 and 1965 if an investor had acted quickly enough in response to quarterly earnings reports, implying, therefore, that the market is inefficient by virtue of its failure to adjust prices instantaneously to the information.

To appreciate why these findings are insufficient to constitute a serious challenge to the market's efficiency, two aspects of the study need to be stressed:

(i)   The abnormal returns were restricted to the period 1962–5. No statistically significant results were observed in the period 1965–8.

(ii) The abnormal returns during the period 1962–5 were insufficient to cover the transaction costs of the ordinary investor.

It follows that:

(a)   The results of the first period may not have amounted to an *authentic* inefficiency, but may have been due to chance.

(b) If an authentic inefficiency really did exist, it appears to have failed the *persistence* criterion, since it could not be relied upon to be effective after 1965. The market possibly 'learnt a lesson'.

(c) Even if the investor had anticipated the inefficiency in 1962 and was in a position to exploit the three years ahead, the alleged inefficiency fails on the *materiality* criterion, since the ordinary investor would not have earned enough to cover transaction costs.

Therefore, although the results are of some concern to researchers, there is no reason to believe that the study of quarterly earnings reports can on the whole be expected to generate abnormal returns for investors.

(2) *Price-Earnings Ratio as a Predictive Tool*

The second case study exemplifies the problems of establishing an authentic inefficiency. More particularly, it highlights the difficulties in interpreting the returns on risky securities unless the model used for testing purposes captures all factors relevant to the measurement of return and risk.

A number of empirical studies dating from 1960[2] through to as recently as 1981[3] have been interpreted to imply that the market is persistently inefficient with respect to Price-Earnings ratios. Portfolios composed of low P/E stocks have been repeatedly found to outperform portfolios of high P/E stocks, after making the conventional adjustments for risk. Indeed, several writers and advisers explicitly advocate an investment strategy based primarily on the relatively simple criterion of restricting selection to low P/E ratio stocks,[4] commonly attributing the phenomenon to a persistent tendency by the market to be overoptimistic in valuing growth stocks.

The validity of the alleged inefficiency, however, is seriously suspect when two additional, quite distinct, factors are considered, both of which have the effect of making the traditional measures of security performance seem quite inadequate in the context. These are:

The Small Firm Effect. Research has shown that P/E and firm size are strongly correlated, small firms being associated with lower P/E ratios than large firms. Reinganum[5] has gone so far as to demonstrate that the so-called P/E effect actually disappears when returns are adjusted for firm size, and argues as a consequence that, whatever explanation is required, it has to do, not with P/E ratios, but with the fact that the shares of small firms appear to earn more than those of large firms of comparable risk. One possible explanation offered by Roll[6] is that the firm size effect may be due to a tendency for standard risk estimates to understate the riskiness of small firms by failing to take account of their infrequent trading characteristics. Subsequent tests[7] have shown that this bias in the risk estimates does appear to exist although not to the extent that would fully explain the small firm effect.

The Tax Effect. In a recent paper, Oppenheimer and Schlarbaum[8] argued that the size factor could not entirely explain away the P/E phenomenon, because they found that a portfolio composed of large companies with low P/E ratios could be shown to earn excess returns, although of significantly lower proportions than a portfolio of comparable small firms. This leads to the second factor with potential relevance to the debate, the controversial issue of how taxation affects security yields.

In addition to their association with firm size, P/E ratios are associated with dividend payout ratios, and this raises the possibility that the P/E phenomenon may be tied up with the controversial, and as yet unresolved issue of whether, and how far, personal taxes impact on security returns. Some writers argue that, just as UK Government bond yields are perceptibly influenced by the differential tax rates between capital gains and ordinary income, so will equity returns. If this is the case, and there is some evidence to support such a tax effect,[9] there may be some link between the market's observed price earnings ratios and personal tax anomalies which has not been fully deciphered.

It is clear, then, that the combination of these two factors—the effect of size on risk and the effect of tax on yield—is sufficient to cast serious doubt on the claim that shares are inefficiently priced with respect to their Price-Earnings ratios. Even on the basis of the accumulated evidence to date, it is arguably no less reasonable to conclude that the P/E phenomenon bears witness to the possibility that the market is considerably more sensitive to the finer dimensions of valuation than it is generally given credit for. Certainly, it confirms the desirability of searching for one or more possible missing factors before concluding that any apparent anomaly persisting over a prolonged period of time is due to a market inefficiency.

(3) *Inflation Accounting as a Predictive Tool*

The third study exemplifies the ease with which observed price movements can be incorrectly interpreted as fulfilments of investors' predictions. A report published in 1981 by Thompson on behalf of London stockbrokers de Zoete and Bevan claimed to contain evidence that throws 'into question the whole concept of the efficient market hypothesis which has been propounded by academics'.[10]

The study argued that a relatively simple predictive tool had been developed, derived from the impact of current cost accounting methods on reported earnings. Companies were graded into five portfolios, ranging from portfolio A comprising those shares which would be least affected by the change to current cost accounting, to portfolio E, those which are most likely to be affected. In 1975 the brokers forecast that between 1975 and 1979 'the earnings of shares in grades D and E will fall materially by comparison with those in grades A and B'. The share price movements of the five portfolios over subsequent years were then traced and, in particular, over the period between April 1977 and January 1981, the results of which are reported in Figure 5.1. The authors concluded that current cost accounting is a useful tool for 'separating the sheep from the goats'.

This argument, however, is analogous to stating that because ice-cream manufacturers can be expected to perform well during dry, hot summers and umbrella manufacturers badly, this observation constitutes a valid predictive tool. The real problem, however, is to determine not how the weather affects individual companies, but how to predict the weather itself. Similarly, in the context of the alleged predictive power of inflation-adjusted accounts, it is necessary to distinguish between:

(a) predicting how the reported earnings of specific companies will be affected by inflation; and

(b) predicting the future rate of inflation itself.

Both sets of data are needed to be able to predict future share prices. As the study itself admits, it is a relatively simple matter to classify companies in terms of the sensitivity of their earnings to inflation. It is another thing to use this classification to produce significantly improved investment performance.

In order to profit from such a classification, it is no less necessary to be able to achieve the second of the two steps above—that is, to out-guess the market in predicting future rates of inflation. A reasonably efficient market will make an estimate of future rates of inflation and will then discount the prices of shares accordingly. If the actual rate experienced equals the rate expected by the market, the subsequent performance of

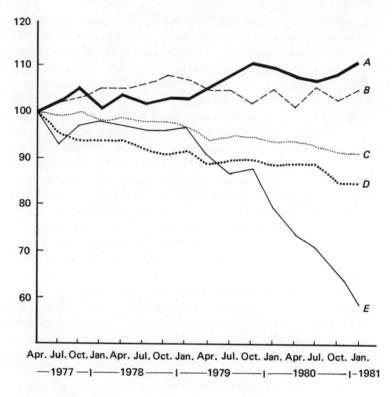

Figure 5.1   *Performance of current cost grading
portfolios relative to FT actuaries industrial index
Source:* de Zoete and Bevan

the respective portfolios should not differ materially. If the actual rate
exceeds the expected rate, the respective portfolios will perform according to the results exhibited in Figure 5.1. If the actual rate is less than
expected, the reverse order should occur.

It happens that the period 1977 to 1981 was a period of severe inflation
in the UK. The relative performance of the five portfolios is therefore
quite consistent with the fact that the rate of inflation exceeded general
expectations. If the authors could demonstrate that they had devised a
tool which allowed them to make superior predictions of the rate of inflation, then it is *that* tool rather than the classification into current cost

gradings which could be held out as throwing the efficient market hypothesis into question. But the paper does not make such a claim. Indeed, it emphasises that the predictive tool is derived directly from the published accounts of the companies in question. But being able to classify companies in respect of their likely reaction to certain events is insufficient to provide the basis of predicting those events.

It might be argued, of course, that the market was inefficient for not making a better prediction of future inflation than it did, and, therefore, for not discounting the respective benefits and disadvantages of inflation earlier. But, to be efficient, the market does not need to be clairvoyant. The issue is whether, from the political and economic signals at the time, the market's estimate of inflation was a reasonable one. This can only be determined by showing that those who claim otherwise are able consistently to produce superior estimates of inflation.

Finally, it could be argued that the above results were caused by a slow market reaction to the effects of inflation and not by the fact that the rate of inflation was higher than expected. If the rate of inflation during the four years in question had been readily predictable, an efficient market should have discounted the effects and adjusted the prices accordingly at the base point (April 1977), with the result that the share price performance of the five portfolios thereafter ought not to have differed materially. The results actually depicted would in that case suggest that the market was inefficient, since it took at least four years to react fully. But it would suggest that the market was more than just a little inefficient, that it was indeed grossly inefficient, so much so that the opportunities for making abnormally high gains would have been enormous. But a number of studies have specifically demonstrated that not only does the market adjust its prices rapidly for expected levels of inflation, but can successfully 'see through' the accounts of most companies that do not prepare current cost accounts.[11]

In summary, the most likely explanation of the results depicted in Figure 5.1 is that they confirm the relatively straightforward fact that during periods of *unexpected* levels of inflation, the shares of certain types of companies perform better than others. This, however, does not in any way throw into question market efficiency. To do that it would be necessary to demonstrate that it is possible consistently to out-guess the market in terms of estimated future rates of inflation and for that no evidence has been produced.

Other Anomalies

Clearly, it is not possible to examine every study containing an anomaly, but the examples that are held out as potential evidence against efficiency are frequently insubstantial in terms of their operational significance insofar as the results, in many cases, fail to satisfy one or more of the exploitability criteria necessary to justify abandoning the passive strategy associated with efficiency. However, in a few cases, the findings appear so unequivocal that no apparent explanation other than inefficiency yet presents itself.

For example, a recent study[12] of earnings forecasts issued by leading US brokerage houses indicated that not only did these appear to have valid information content, but that the market's response to their publication was sufficiently slow to have enabled investors to trade profitably on the signals they contained, even when transaction costs were taken into account.

In 1978, Chiras and Manaster[13] reported an inefficiency of sufficiently consistent magnitude in the Chicago Board Options Exchange during the period June 1973 to April 1975 to allow a trade in options using a specific strategy to have earned significantly higher than average returns. In another study relating to the information content of dividend changes, Charest[14] found that during the period 1947–67, the New York Stock Exchange under-reacted to dividend change announcements sufficiently to allow an investor trading in the stocks around the time of the declarations to earn significantly abnormal returns. A few other studies have produced equally anomalous results.[15]

The operational significance of these findings has to be viewed, however, in the perspective of the total body of evidence. Even if they are genuine, they do not prove market inefficiency in any general sense. The findings are very specific and there is no spillover to other potential inefficiencies. Hence, financial advisers or exponents of some particular strategy or other cannot point, say, to the Charest study as validation of a general state of inefficiency justifying their own claim to provide superior profits. Any such claim must stand or fall on its own merits independently of the market's observed reaction to change of dividend announcements.

In addition, there is no evidence that the apparent inefficiencies were explicitly recognised as such by investors during the period under review. The fact that they could have been exploited is itself of limited significance. Without the actual corroboration of reseach, the systematic exploitation of dividend announcements, for example, would have been only one strategy among many that could have been followed in good faith with little reason at the time to believe that it would be any more successful than the rest. Therefore, even if one believes that a small proportion of the many trading rules on offer in the market at any given time is likely to be successful, this confidence is of little practical significance until the successful strategies are identified and distinguished from the rest.

It follows that the operationality of such inefficiencies depends, in the last analysis, on the market's response to their exposure. For the investor to be able to beat-the-market systematically, the market must not only be errant, it must be obstinately so. Therefore, before jettisoning the basic hold-the-market policy of efficient market theory, the investor has to judge whether it is reasonable to expect publicly authenticated trading rules to survive the scrutiny and attention of professional analysts.

There is, however, one prominent example of an alleged inefficiency which appears to possess all the characteristics of exploitability, because, despite publicity, it has persisted over a considerable period of time, and is accessible to the ordinary investor, namely the Value Line system.[16] This is a complex investment model which has long had the reputation in the US of being able to achieve superior returns.

Details of the system are not made available to the public, but the key components include (1) the relationship of last year's earnings and share price to the past 10 years' experience, (2) relative Price-Earnings ratio performances, (3) 'earnings momentum', the relationship of current earnings to previous years' comparable earnings, and (4) 'earnings surprise', the relationship of recent quarterly earnings with prior estimates of Value Line analysts.[17] It is, therefore, a system based on a composite of judgmental and objective rules, but the ordinary investor can gain access to the system through funds based on the Value Line system.

The major relevant research study is that by Black[18] which indicated that over a period of years, VL had a fairly consistent ability to detect undervalued securities, although their findings were subsequently rejected by Kaplan and Weil.[19] In a more recent study, Holloway found that by following VL's recommendations as a basis for an active trading strategy, it was not possible to generate enough excess returns to cover transaction costs.[20] However, he did find that with a buy-and-hold policy using VL recommendations, an investor could earn better returns than a buy-and-hold-the-market policy. Against that, it has been noted that VL rankings are to some extent based on P/E strategies,[21] and the problem of assessing their apparent success is consequently closely tied up with the issues previously discussed under P/E ratios. It is possible, therefore, that the phenomenon is at least partly a manifestation of the unresolved size and taxation factors.

The research studies are, therefore, inconclusive about Value Line. Whilst the indications are that an active strategy based on VL recommendations is unlikely to be profitable, it would seem that unless the P/E phenomenon or some other factor provides an explanation for VL's performance, there may be some benefit in adopting a passive strategy based on Value Line selections.

Market Timing and the Efficiency of Prices in Aggregate

It is argued by some that even if the market is able by and large to price its securities correctly relative to one another, the general price level of shares is apt at times to go adrift, and that this offers investors the opportunity to time their transactions in the market in such a way as to defeat the pure buy-and-hold strategy of efficient market theory. For example, 1974 is cited as an illustration of how the market portfolio itself can be significantly mispriced. During that year the *Financial Times* 30 share index fell to around 160 compared to a level well above 500 some few years before, a differential which would of course be significantly greater if expressed in a common monetary value. Some commentators claimed at the time, and certainly since, that the general market level had as a result become exceedingly 'cheap'. Whether this judgment was based on a comparison of the estimated future return from the UK market portfolio with the then current risk-free rate or with the estimated future returns from other national markets is not clear, but the problems of testing such a claim are significant.

Verification of the correctness of the general level of security prices at a particular point in time presents similar kinds of difficulties as those identified in Chapter 2 in verifying the correctness of individual security prices, plus some additional problems. Whilst evaluation of individual securities involves a determination of the consistency with which securities are priced *vis-à-vis* one another, given the price of risk ruling at the time, evaluation of the general level of prices calls for an additional judgment about the appropriateness of the price of risk itself. Since very little is known of the process or the factors which determine the magnitude of the ruling price of risk, this must remain an exceedingly speculative judgment.

1974, for instance, happened to include a period of intense economic and political uncertainty, when for a period of time there were serious discussions in the press about the possibility of a partial collapse of the capitalist sytem in the UK. If the political risks were as severe as some suggested, it was right for the market to have incorporated into its probability distribution the possibility of dire consequences for security values, however far removed such a possibility might appear to many investors. How then, in that peculiar set of circumstances, is one to assess the validity of the claim that the market had 'got its odds wrong'? Certainly not by simple reference to the subsequent course of the market index, since the point has already been established that the efficiency of pricing decisions cannot be measured by what happens after the uncertainties have been resolved. It might be possible to discover a tendency for the market to over-react in such circumstances by studying a statistically significant number of similar events to determine whether investors who claim to have superior macroeconomic insights succeed in outperforming a simple buy-and-hold strategy. But since the intensity of the political uncertainty in 1974 was of a rare quality, finding a sufficient number of similar occurrences clearly presents a problem. Even if these could be found, and a tendency to over-react was confirmed, it would always remain a matter of speculation whether the market had over-reacted in the particular set of circumstances of 1974.

Some would argue that there is no need for investors to depend on such rare and dramatic circumstances to exploit the market because the movements in the market index present sufficient opportunity for informed interpreters of macroeconomic conditions to enter and quit the market portfolio profitably at regular intervals. Certainly it is tempting to view the troughs and peaks of the market's past performances as signalling clear opportunities for profitable timing. One writer, for instance, observes:

> 'EMH states that nothing is to be gained by attempting to time moves into or out of the stock market ... A study of stock markets shows that markets tend to spend about one-third of the time over-anticipating subsequent results, about one-third in reacting downwards from over-anticipation, about one-fifth moving indecisively at the top or bottom of the cyclical pattern and about one-fifth of the time moving in the direction and at a rate which would be justified by a rational assessment of future prospects. EMH ignores the impact of over-anticipation.'[22]

But it needs more than the perceptions of hindsight to confirm that the market's observed turning points provide identifiable buy-sell signals. Much of the research into the weak form of market efficiency has dispelled the notion that the market moves in predictable patterns, at either the individual security or the aggregate level. As for the assertion that the market regularly and perceptibly over-reacts to publicly available information, this may simply underline the relatively incomplete and myopic vision of the individual observer compared to that of the market. There is certainly very little evidence to suggest that investors can successfully exploit the movements of the market portfolio with sufficient margin to cover the transaction costs. Amongst the direct evidence, one study by Umstead[23] in the United States suggested that a successful trading rule could be derived based on the Leading Composite Index, a business activity indicator published by the National Bureau of Economic Research. The study claimed that movements in the general level of stock prices could be predicted from the LCI sufficiently accurately to outperform a passive, buy-and-hold policy. The author himself speculated that such an inefficiency could have resulted from a failure by investors hitherto to employ the complex statistical techniques used to identify the relationship and that as the technology becomes more widely utilised, the advantage attached to the trading rule would disappear.

However, there is some doubt about the validity of Umstead's primary conclusions. Significant statistical deficiencies in the research were subsequently revealed both by Whitcomb[24] and Arzac[25] which raised serious doubts about the conclusion that a successful trading rule had been devised. Furthermore, some other studies support the opposing view, indicating, for example, that the market successfully anticipates changes in government monetary policy.[26]

There is a recent body of literature which has sought to investigate directly the notion that security prices are too volatile to accord with efficient market theory.[27] This notion is based on the observation that share prices appear to vary considerably more than is appropriate for the observed variability of related dividend streams, implying an over-reaction by the market to information about future dividends. However, it is not clear what conclusions can validly be drawn from these studies. Any attempt to provide an adequate definition of the limits of price volatility that can be reconciled with market efficiency is heavily dependent on the ability to construct a comprehensive model of security prices behaviour. The model used by Shiller was acknowledged by necessity to be restrictive and, therefore, his findings are not inconsistent with other explanations besides market inefficiency. In addition, even if security price volatility is assumed to be excessive, and indicative of faddish

behaviour by investors, it was not suggested that an exploitable inefficiency had necessarily been identified for investors who were not
vulnerable to the fads. Therefore, considerably more understanding of
the factors that determine the value of the market portfolio of risky assets
is necessary before any significant conclusions can be drawn about
observed changes in that value.

The indirect evidence adds further support to the conclusion that
'market timing' is not a profitable exercise given the round-trip costs.
Sharpe[28] found that to profit from the decision whether to hold cash or
the market portfolio it was necessary to be right nearly four out of five
times. A similar test of the Belgian market[29] indicated the need to be
right as much as nine out of ten times. Finally, tests of professional fund
managers' ability to achieve success in this respect have indicated the
absence of any consistent timing skill.[30]

There is no valid reason, therefore, to believe that the movements of
the market index are any more predictable than those of individual
stocks. The market's efficiency appears to apply no less to prices in aggregate than to individual securities, confirming the optimality of a buy-and-
hold policy.

Market Tests and Problems in Methodology

Recently, the debate has focused on certain problems inherent in the
research methodology employed in efficient market tests. The purpose
of this section is not to review in detail the technical aspects of these
problems, but to consider the implications for the ordinary investor of
the simple fact that they exist. It has been argued that, to be effective, the
evidence has to be gathered and collated by trained researchers, but the
fact remains that the findings have to be evaluated by the ordinary
investor faced with the practical problem of choosing between an active
and a passive strategy. In the end, he has to decide whether or not the
market is efficient for him. How then is he to make this decision if an
element of doubt hangs over the validity of the researcher's methods?

The source of the problem is in the method of controlling for risk, an
essential step in the process of interpreting investment results. For
example, without some appropriate adjustment, it is not possible to compare confidently the performance of a specific fund with that of the
market, if the respective risks are different. The general principle that

greater risk should carry greater expected reward is not sufficiently specific to enable a researcher to judge how great a reward is required to compensate for the difference in risk.

The most elaborate and widely accepted theory for explaining the relationship between risk and return is the Capital Asset Pricing Model (CAPM) of Sharpe, Lintner and others,[31] which briefly states that the risk premium on an individual asset is a function of the covariability of the asset's returns with the returns on the market portfolio of all risky assets.[32] This model will be considered more fully in subsequent chapters. The CAPM has been widely used as the vehicle for adjusting for risk in empirical tests for efficiency, but some serious doubts about the validity of its use in all circumstances were raised by Richard Roll in 1977.[33] This paper has been commonly referred to since its publication simply as the *Roll critique*. The problem arises principally because of the difficulty in practice of specifying the precise composition of the 'market portfolio', which is a key concept in the tests used by the researcher, being the benchmark by which the risk class of individual securities and portfolios is determined. Roll pointed out that because the market portfolio can never properly be identified, and because, as a result, researchers have to use a proxy for the market (such as the Dow Jones Industrial Average), the benchmark used for measuring risk in practice can never be wholly reliable. The research findings, therefore, have to be evaluated in the light of this criticism.

The initial reaction to Roll's paper was one of alarm because it seemed to raise the possibility that the entire body of accumulated research from which EMH evolved was, after all, built on a relatively sandy structure. Fortunately, however, subsequent debate in the journal literature has placed the issue in better perspective.

To begin with, it needs to be stressed that Roll's critique of CAPM does not imply that the model is invalid, or that the market is inefficient. The problems concern the testability of CAPM and its relevance as a vehicle for testing the market's efficiency. The implication is that market tests of efficiency which make direct use of CAPM have to be treated with some caution, though to what extent is unclear.

Moreover, the problems do not apply equally to the two approaches employed in testing market efficiency, the direct approach of studying the reaction of securities to certain economic events, and the indirect approach of studying the performance of professional investors against some recognisable yardstick. In a subsequent comment on Roll's paper, Mayers and Rice[34] pointed out that his criticism did not really apply to the former set of tests. Roll conceded the point[35] and accepted that the issue relates primarily to performance evaluation. However, since it is on the basis of the indirect evidence that much of the positive case for EMH rests, Roll's paper is still a matter of potential significance.

Attempts have been made by some writers recently to measure this significance for performance evaluation analysis. For example, a study by Peterson and Rice in 1980[36] tested the sensitivity of the results of portfolio evaluation to different indices used as proxies for the market portfolio and found no systematic difference in the findings. They concluded that, despite the theoretical shortcomings, 'little serious injustice is committed' in the use of traditional portfolio evaluation tools. And again, in another study by Peasnell, Skerratt and Taylor,[37] the Jensen investigation into mutual fund performance reported in Chapter 4 was reworked using the insights of arbitrage theory,[38] and this exercise appeared to provide independent confirmation of Jensen's findings that professionally managed funds are unable systematically to outperform the market. However, the PST study has been subsequently criticised in a paper which seriously challenges the possibility of using arbitrage concepts to circumvent the problems inherent in performance measurement.[39]

Some serious doubt, therefore, does remain about the robustness of traditional efficiency testing procedures, as indeed there is with respect to most econometric models. How is the layman investor to interpret the evidence when the validity of the tools used to collect it are open to question? Clearly this is a difficult issue, but at least it can be assumed that the problems of evidence gathering have potentially more serious consequences for the active investment school than for passive investors. The onus of proof is to show that exploitable inefficiencies exist, and, to do so, it is necessary to have a valid methodology for gathering and assessing evidence. If, at the extreme, all past tests were rejected because of deficiencies in their methodology, then, although this would destroy the accumulated evidence favouring efficiency, it would also destroy any evidence favouring inefficiency. More important, it would leave the active strategists in the position of having to construct a methodology powerful enough to initiate a new stream of research to enable them to discharge their onus. In the meantime, for reasons already given, economic self-interest would favour investors behaving as if the market were efficient.

It is unlikely that anyone would seriously argue that the above problems are sufficient to invalidate all previous research. Most writers seem to take the view that we should at worst regard the results with some caution, whatever that may signify. What is important, however, is that for all the potential defects of current methodology, the accumulated results do point mainly in one direction. It is a matter of speculation whether the absence of those defects would produce any significantly different indications.

Some Criticisms of the Case Presented for Efficiency

Efficient market writers are commonly critical of the conventional viewholder on the grounds that his case is often anecdotal and unscientific. The former, however, have themselves not escaped criticism. Hatjoullis,[40] and others[41] argue that EMH writers are guilty of a number of tendencies:

(a) they tend to attribute anomalous results to mis-specification of the model rather than to concede an inefficiency;

(b) they assume that the market will learn from its mistakes;

(c) they tend to overstate the significance of trading costs in assessing the impact of reported anomalies.

The present writer is guilty, in part at least, of using all three arguments and, therefore, some comment is appropriate.

(a) *Model Mis-Specification*

There is undoubtedly a tendency for proponents of both sides of the argument, when approaching the evidence, to be influenced by their prior beliefs. Conventional writers appear to demand what the other side perceive to be an impossible and unnecessary task—conclusive proof of EMH before it should be considered as operationally valid. They would presumably defend this view on the grounds that the received wisdom is too established to be overturned without overwhelming evidence. By way of contrast, those who are sympathetic with the concept of efficiency, given the competitive and professional nature of the market, tend to accept the favourable evidence readily and to be somewhat critical of the methodological procedures in the studies that conflict with EMH. It is arguable that this apparently inconsistent behaviour is not without justification on the grounds that it is natural for a more rigorous standard to be exacted from evidence favouring the side on which the onus of proof is assumed to rest. All possible avenues should be explored before an alleged inefficiency is accepted as authentic and deserving of an investor's commitment of capital, and the natural place to initiate such a search is in the testing procedures, to seek out any missing factor with potential explanatory power.

Hatjoullis also notes that certain EMH researchers are given to arguing that a recognised anomaly which has persisted for some time is all the more likely to be due to a model mis-specification than to an inefficiency.[42] This argument, of course, is defended on the grounds that, given the competitive nature of the market, it is likely that an inefficiency known to provide superior profits would be rapidly seized by investors and fairly quickly priced out of existence.

The inclination to blame the model, therefore, arises because tests of the market are essentially tests of a joint hypothesis, the hypothesis that the market is efficient, and the hypothesis that the model of the market is valid. The extent to which EMH writers are guilty of this tendency reflects the fact that they have probably greater faith in the concept of a competitive market than they have in their model of the market.

(b) *The Market's Learning Skill*

The final argument in the preceding section, that any significant inefficiency revealed by research is likely to be rapidly priced away is, of course, itself criticised by opponents as a Catch 22 argument.[43] But, if one accepts that the overall evidence suggests at least that exploitable inefficiencies are difficult to unearth, then it is not an unreasonable assumption, given the problems experienced by fund managers in achieving above-average results, and the competitive pressures under which they operate, that any proven investment technique would be quickly adopted and its efficiency in time defeated. It would be inconsistent with the evidence supporting the market's rapid responsiveness to new information that it should be otiose in assimilating the lessons contained in any investment strategy known to have been successful in the past.

(c) *Overstating the Significance of Trading Costs*

The final criticism against EMH writers, namely that they tend to exaggerate the importance of trading costs, is based on two observations:

1. Although trading costs would be incurred if an investor had to switch his current holdings to pursue a specific inefficiency, many investors are faced with a continuing inflow of investment funds which, if used in executing a particular investment strategy, would not involve any incremental trading costs.[44] That is, the set-up costs of one portfolio are not necessarily greater than another, and trading costs, therefore, should not deter the investor initially from taking advantage of any marginal opportunity for abnormal gain. Even if the market is too efficient to warrant incurring the trading costs of an active investment strategy, it may be inefficient enough to warrant selecting and passively holding a particular subset of the market, since this entails no additional transaction costs compared to holding the market portfolio advocated by theory. This solution may possibly be valid, but it needs to be recognised that, unless the alleged inefficiency is widespread, restricting investment to marginally mispriced securities will probably lead to inefficient diversification. It is doubtful that inefficiencies which do not provide enough excess profit to cover trading costs will provide enough profit to compensate for an imperfectly diversified position. Finally, it should also be noted that unless the marginal inefficiency is continuously on offer, the excess profit must be sufficient to justify forfeiting the income lost in delaying investment until the inefficiency reappears.

2. A number of research studies have focused on the predictive power of a single item of information, dismissing the item if its utilisation does not cover the costs of trading. In practice, however, an investor is likely to use a combination of information items, and since the trading costs have only to be paid once, it is argued that it is misleading to charge all the trading costs to the item being researched.[45]

One cannot quarrel with the principle that a combination of different types of information may have potentially more predictive power than a single item, and it is true that the research literature is deficient in tests of combined items. However, there are practical difficulties in testing combined sources of information, and until a specific combination is identified that has forecasting potential and is also testable, one can only observe that the evidence relating to the performance of expertly managed funds has failed to indicate that professional managers, who can be assumed to combine a wide variety of information sources in their selection process, are able to achieve a net gain after transaction costs.

Conclusion

The empirical evidence relating to the market's pricing efficiency is composed of a massive body of findings substantially supportive of efficiency, plus a relatively small number of enigmas which for the main part are either fairly insignificant in economic terms or appear capable of being explained with finer analysis, and finally a few stubborn contradictions which hitherto have defied satisfactory explanation.

What conclusions can be drawn? If the concept of efficiency is recognised for what it is, that is not an all-or-nothing state analogous to the credibility of a witness whose entire testimony is destroyed by a single proven perjury, but a matter of degree ranging from gross inefficiency to perfect efficiency, then there is little doubt that the market must be judged to be highly efficient. The popular notion that abnormal profits can readily be earned either by reasonable diligence or by entrusting one's investment policy to a competent professional adviser is far from consistent with the evidence. Only one of two conclusions can be drawn, that it makes no economic sense for investors, apart from a limited number of highly skilled arbitrageurs, to base their investment strategy on any assumption other than that the market is efficient, or alternatively that it is possibly worthwhile to exploit any inefficiencies that research happens to have unearthed.

The debate, therefore, is not between efficiency and inefficiency. It is between efficiency and the possible inefficiency of the Chicago Options Market, or the possible inefficiency with respect to dividend changing stocks, or whatever other inefficiency might be verified. The choices are few and very specific. The onus of proof that resides with the active investment school is not discharged if one or two inefficiencies are authenticated. Each potential inefficiency presented for active consideration has to be individually validated before it acquires operational significance.

But if an active strategy is to be pursued, it must be founded on what can only be an act of faith, namely that the market, for all its remarkable efficiency, and for all its competitiveness, is too obstinate to react rationally to the discovery of its own imperfections. It is this act of faith, of course, that underscores the difference in the prior beliefs of the two schools of thought, the traditional conviction that visible opportunities are almost certain to present themselves to the perceptive investor, and the economist's belief in the efficacy of competition to consume any such opportunities that emerge. It is this writer's belief that the cumulative evidence has overwhelmingly corroborated the view of the economist.

Problems such as those identified in this chapter have been interpreted by some as calling for a not proven verdict on the issue.[46] But if the onus of proof rests on the side of inefficiency, then even a not proven verdict implies that the case for behaving as if the market is near efficient is an inescapable one. That is, there do not appear to be any rule-of-thumb inefficiencies which allow investors systematically to beat the market, and, to the extent that there are judgmental inefficiencies, these tend to be perceptible only to skilled experts. An outstanding illustration of this concept of near efficiency is provided by the market's reaction to the published articles of Abraham Briloff, a noted and highly respected critic of corporate accounting practices.[47] The evidence indicates that the shares of companies criticised by Briloff drop in price on average by 8% on the day his article is published. Although several interpretations of this reaction have been presented,[48] two important aspects of the phenomenon illustrate the sense in which the market can be viewed as near efficient:

(a) The analyses by Briloff are exceptionally sophisticated, and although apparently based on publicly available information sources, the insights he provides cannot readily be regarded as having been part of the information set generally available to the investment community. The results are consistent with the notion that a few analysts with specially gifted insights can in a sense create new information and earn economic rents from their information production activity.

(b) The market's reactions to his announcements are rapid, and consistent with the conclusion that the insights of the expert are effectively non-transmittible to the general investor. The gifted analyst is analogous to the privileged insider whose communications to the market form an integral part of the public information set.

Sceptics might sense a devastating inevitability in the arguments favouring market efficiency. First, evidence is presented that experts are on average unable to perform better than the market, implying that the market's prices are efficient. If any investors appear to perform better, they do so only because their portfolios are more risky than the market. If some perform even better than their risk exposure warrants, they earn sufficient only to cover their trading and search costs. If research should disclose the existence of an investment technique capable of generating superior returns in excess of trading costs, the market would 'learn' from the experience and rapidly price away any benefit from using the technique. Finally, if the research technology used to establish the above findings can be shown to be deficient in any serious respect, then this will diminish significantly the possibility of the traditional camp ever being able to discharge its burden of validating the existence of even a single exploitable inefficiency.

The apparent intractability of this sequence of arguments may appear to place proponents of the conventional view in something of a straitjacket. There is no doubt that it underlines a fundamental and inescapable conclusion about the entire question of market efficiency, namely the complete lack of justification for the general presumption of inefficiency that characterises the conventional stance, and the enormity of the task facing those who seek to validate that presumption.

Notes and References

1. Watts, R.L. (1978) 'Systematic abnormal returns after quarterly earnings announcements', *Journal of Financial Economics*, September.
2. Nicholson, S.F. (1960) 'Price-earnings ratios', *Financial Analysts Journal*, July/August.
3. Oppenheimer, H. and Schlarbaum, G. (1981) 'Investing with Ben Graham: an *ex ante* test of the efficient markets hypothesis', *Journal of Financial and Quantitative Analysis*, September.
4. For example, Dreman, D. (1977) *Psychology and the Stock Market*, Amocom, 1977 and Graham, B. (1973) *The Intelligent Investor*, New York, Harper & Row.
5. Reinganum, M. (1981b) 'Misspecification of capital asset pricing: empirical anomalies based on earnings' yields and market values', *Journal of Financial Economics*, March.
6. Roll, R. (1981) 'A possible explanation of the small firm effect', *Journal of Finance*, September.
7. Reinganum, M. (1982) 'A direct test of Roll's conjecture on the firm size effect', *Journal of Finance*, March.
8. *op. cit.*
9. Litzenberger, R.H. and Ramaswamy, K. (1982) 'The effects of dividends on common stock prices: tax effects or information effects?', *Journal of Finance*, May. Note that for a more subtle and speculative explanation of the P/E anomaly see the 'Discussion' on the above paper by Summers (1982) *Journal of Finance*, May, who argues that the higher returns associated with high yield securities may be the result of undetected changes in risk, bringing about a fall in value in the securities, and therefore leading to higher yields. That is, higher yields are a *result* rather than a *cause* of higher expected returns.

74 STOCK MARKET EFFICIENCY

10. Thompson, A.P. (1981) 'Inflation accounting has helped share selections' *Investment Analyst*, October.
11. For example, see Easman, W., Falkenstein, A., Weil, R. and Guy, D. (1979) 'The correlation between sustainable income and stock returns', *Financial Analysts Journal*, September/October.
12. Givoly, D. and Lakonishok, J. (1979) 'The information content of financial analysts' forecasts of earnings: some evidence on semi-strong inefficiency', *Journal of Financial Economics*, December.
13. Chiras, D. and Manaster, S. (1978) 'The information content of option prices and a test of market efficiency', *Journal of Financial Economics*, September.
14. Charest, G. (1978) 'Dividend information, stock returns and market efficiency', *Journal of Financial Economics*, September.
15. See, for example, the entire issue of *Journal of Financial Economics* (1978) September.
16. Bernhard, A. (1975) *Investing in Common Stocks*, New York, Arnold Bernhard and Co.
17. See Sharpe, W. (1981) *Investments*, Prentice-Hall, pp.407–9.
18. Black, F. (1973) 'Yes Virginia, there is hope: tests of value line ranking system', *Financial Analysts Journal*, September/October.
19. Kaplan, R.S. and Weil, R.L. (1973) 'Rejoinder to Fisher Black', *Financial Analysts Journal*, July.
20. Holloway, C. (1981) 'A note on testing an aggressive investment strategy using value line ranks', *Journal of Finance*, June.
21. See Ball, R. (1978) 'Anomalies in relationships between yields and yield-surrogates', *Journal of Financial Economics*, June/September.
22. Donnelly, A. (1980) 'Why relative cost is a better basis for investment decisions than the "efficient market" fallacy', *The Chartered Accountant in Australia*, May.
23. Umstead, D. (1977) 'Forecasting stock market prices', *Journal of Finance*, May.
24. Whitcomb, D. (1977) 'Discussion', *Journal of Finance*, May.
25. Arzac, E. (1977) 'Discussion', *Journal of Finance*, May.
26. Cooper, R. (1974) 'Efficient capital markets and the quantity theory of money', *Journal of Finance*, June.
27. Shiller, R. (1981a & b) 'The use of volatility measures in assessing market efficiency', *Journal of Finance*, May, and 'Do stock prices move too much to be justified by subsequent changes in dividends?' *American Economic Review*, June. Also see Long J.B. Jr. (1981) 'Discussion' *Journal of Finance*, May.
28. Sharpe, W. (1975) 'Are gains likely from market timing?' *Financial Analysts Journal*, March/April.
29. Farber, A. (1976) 'National and international market timing strategies', Commission on Practical Fund Management, 9th Congress, European Federation of Financial Analysts Societies, May.
30. See discussion by Henfrey, A., Albrecht, B. and Richards, P. (1977) 'The UK stock market and the efficient market model', *Investment Analyst*, September, p. 17.

31. Sharpe, W. (1964) 'Capital asset prices: a theory of market equilibrium under conditions of risk, *Journal of Finance*, September, and Lintner, J. (1965) 'Security policies, risk and maximal gains from diversification', *Journal of Finance*, December.
32. See Foster, *op.cit.* pp. 246–7.
33. Roll, R. (1977) 'A critique of the asset pricing theory's tests, part 1: on past and potential testability of the theory', *Journal of Financial Economics*, March.
34. Mayers, D. and Rice, E. (1979) 'Measuring portfolio performance and the empirical content of asset pricing models', *Journal of Financial Economics*, March.
35. Roll, R. (1979) 'A reply to Mayers and Rice (1979)' *Journal of Financial Economics*, December.
36. Peterson, D. and Rice, M. (1980) 'A note on ambiguity in portfolio performance measures', *Journal of Finance*, December.
37. Peasnell, K., Skerratt, L. and Taylor, P. (1979) 'An arbitrage rationale for tests of mutual fund performance', *Journal of Business Finance and Accounting*, Autumn.
38. See *ibid.* pp. 380–7.
39. Appleyard, A.R., Strong N. and Walker, M. (1982) 'Mutual fund performance in the context of models of equilbrium capital asset pricing', *Journal of Business Finance and Accounting*, Autumn.
40. Hatjoullis, G.S. (1981) 'The efficient markets hypothesis: a critical overview', Working Paper Series, Manchester Business School.
41. Clarkson, R.S. (1981) 'A market equilibrium model for the management of ordinary share portfolios', Scottish Mutual Assurance Society.
42. *op. cit.* p.12.
43. Clarkson, *op.cit.* p.111.
44. Hatjoullis, *op.cit.* p.14.
45. *Ibid.* p.14.
46. Renwick, F. (1982) 'Discussion paper', *Journal of Finance*, May.
47. e.g. Briloff, A.J. (1974) 'You deserve a break: McDonald's burgers are more palatable than its accounts', *Barron's*, July 6.
48. See Foster, G. (1979) 'Briloff and the capital markets', *Journal of Accounting Research*, Spring.

6

Some Misconceptions

In earlier chapters two distinct sources of evidence were identified, the 'official' research literature and an unofficial source, comprising an unstructured and disparate collection of anecdotes and impressions drawn largely from personal experience. Chapters 4 and 5 were concerned with the first source and this chapter with the second.

It might appear tendentious to label the unofficial body of evidence as a series of misconceptions, particularly when each of the arguments considered in this chapter happens to support the conventional school. But the term misconception is used to denote the type of argument employed, rather than the conclusion drawn from it. Hence any argument which violates the principle that the issue of efficiency can be resolved only by statistical analysis is arguably based on a misconception. This is no less true with respect to arguments supporting efficiency than for those against. For example, it is sometimes asserted that if experts truly knew how to earn above-average returns, they would be unwilling to reveal their methods or to use them to serve the investment interests of others. But this is no less specious an argument than any considered in this chapter, or any other argument of a similar type advanced in support of efficiency.

Certainly, many writers might be inclined to dismiss most of the arguments that follow as straw men simply on the grounds that they invariably fail to address the empirical literature directly. But they are included here because there has long been a tendency to underestimate their practical importance, given that it is these and arguments like them that appear to form the basis of the majority of investors' beliefs. A number of them indeed have a certain superficial appeal and the debate is never likely to be concentrated on the central issues if arguments of the kind continue to be accepted by practitioners as adequate substitutes for the empirical literature. The misconceptions fall into three distinct categories: the nature of market efficiency (sections 1–3), the evidence for efficiency (4–9) and the implications of efficiency (10–14).

The Nature of Efficiency

The first group of misconceptions arises from a misunderstanding of what market efficiency signifies. A near efficient market has been defined as one which captures a particular information set in its security prices in such a way as to prevent all but the most skilful investors from profiting as a result of possessing the same information. If an efficient market is incorrectly interpreted as one which must necessarily be composed of all-knowing and all-seeing investors, who can penetrate the uncertainties of the future, then it is understandable why misconceptions such as the following arise.

1. *Surely, the market cannot always be right*

"The complexities of interpretational problems leave ample room for [the market] to be wrong fairly often.[1] Elsewhere the same writer dismisses efficiency because it implies that 'information is correctly dealt with by [the market] no matter how vague, muddled or difficult'. For example, if the Chairman of Bethlehem Steel says in answer to a reporter's query that the second quarter 'doesn't look too great' and walks away without saying anything more, and the company makes no further comment, [the market] can immediately quantify this statement and arrive at the proper new value for this stock.'[2]

In an earlier chapter the price of a share was likened to a bet placed against possible future states of the world. It was concluded, however, that the correctness of the odds could not be verified in the same way as the odds for a flip of a coin. They are derived from complex probability distributions in which the various possible outcomes in the future are carefully estimated and weighted. Therefore, the accuracy of the odds has to be judged in the light of the information available at the time. But they cannot be judged individually or contemporaneously, only through the retrospective analysis of large samples of 'bets'. If it is found that some investors can consistently do better than average, only then is it possible to infer that the market was incorrect in setting the odds.

Therefore, when an investor asserts that the market price is wrong in a specific set of circumstances, the chances are that (a) he is simply revealing the inadequacy of his own information set versus that of the market, as a basis for interpreting the market's odds, or (b) he is using his subsequent hindsight to conclude that if the market had known at the time what he knows now, it would not have reacted the way it did.

Now, in the example cited above, the author is incorrectly implying that, to be right, the market must be able to see through the vagueness of the Chairman's statement and to be able to react as knowingly as if the statement had been fully informative. In effect, he is suggesting that an efficient market should be able to know what has not been revealed to it. But to be right the market does not have to be either omniscient or clair-voyant. It is sufficient that it makes a reasonable assessment of the probable implications of the Chairman's statement, and adjusts the odds accordingly. The proper value in this context, therefore, relates to the quality of the information received, not to the information that might ideally have been obtained. It is the semi-strong worth, not the strong worth, that is at issue.

In summary, the rightness or wrongness of a share's price cannot be discerned from direct observation, and can never be anything more than an inference drawn from the insights of retrospective statistical enquiry. Such enquiries have tended to indicate that, when setting odds, the market is nearly always right.

2. EMH assumes that all investors behave rationally

'The EMH findings that professionals do not outperform the market ... do not prove the hypothesis that all investors are rational and have equal interpretative capabilities.'[3]

A common difficulty for many critics is to reconcile the market's efficiency with the existence of so many apparently irrational and ill-informed investors. Efficient market writers, however, do not make any assumption that all or even most investors are rational and well-informed. They do not even argue *a priori* that there are a sufficient number of rational investors to make the market efficient. They simply assert that if empirical tests indicate that the market's prices are the best estimate of worth available, then it is a reasonable presumption that there exist a sufficient number of rational and informed investors to have brought this condition about. To this writer's knowledge, no researcher has in fact ever attempted to specify what proportion of investors needs to be rational to make the market efficient. EMH is premised simply on the possibility that the irrational activities of the great mass of investors may generally cancel one another out or, where they do not, that their actions may be compensated for by the intervention of a relatively small number of professional experts. What proportion that number of experts bears to the number of irrational investors is a matter for speculation.

The possibility that market efficiency could hold without relying on the existence and activity of experts is posited by some writers[4] on the assumption that the idiosyncratic behaviour of individual investors may be diversified away in the consensus view. Whilst this argument could explain away the effect of individual investors' prejudices and psychological dispositions, it is unlikely to explain, for example, the market's ability to see through complex accounting numbers. The argument would, however, suggest that the consensus may reflect a superior judgment to that of any of the individual experts who help to determine it.

3. Stock market bubbles imply inefficiency

'Speculative bubbles do occur from time to time and their occurrence (though generally only positively identifiable after the event) is evidence of the existence of period market irrationality.'[5]

The use of an emotive term such as 'speculative bubble' to describe a particular series of share price movements certainly conveys the impression of market irrationality. The real issue, however, is not whether a speculative bubble indicates market inefficiency, but whether the term is a valid description of the particular series of price movements under review. The term certainly reveals what personal interpretation the user places on such a series.

Imagine, for example, that the directors of a small Australian[6] exploration company announce unexpectedly to the market the discovery of a significant deposit of high quality nickel ore, independently certified by reputable geologists. A sizeable and immediate rise in the share price would be viewed as perfectly rational.

If, by way of contrast, the first intimation to the market were a casual remark by a company engineer, followed by a cautious admission by the directors that an indeterminate quantity of reasonable quality ore had been found, then the market's reaction would presumably be cautiously bullish. If, subsequently, due to some extraneous factor, the world price of nickel happened suddenly to rise, and the directors were simultaneously able to announce that the extent of the discovery was materially greater than first supposed, the price of the shares would increase dramatically. If, finally, the geological report later indicated that a high proportion of the ore was in fact low grade and marginally unprofitable to extract, the shares could be expected to tumble.

How should one describe the series of price movements that reflect these events? A speculative bubble, or simply the logical response to a dramatic and somewhat confusing sequence of events? An observer who is not fully aware of the circumstances in which the information was gradually unfolded might dismiss the rise and fall of the share price as market over-reaction. But it is perfectly rational for market prices to respond to potentially important information, even when the credibility of the information is open to dispute, provided the inferior quality of the information is fully allowed for in the process.

Indeed, the above quotation might reasonably be paraphrased 'if the market is known to behave irrationally, then this is evidence of irrationality'. One would clearly have difficulty in arguing with this tautology. The question that should be asked, however, is whether the market is irrational in its response to rumour and to the confused and undisciplined dissemination of price-sensitive information. A clear distinction should be maintained between the efficiency of the securities market and that of the information market. The former may respond quite efficiently to the inefficiencies of the latter.

The Evidence for Efficiency

In Chapter 2, considerable emphasis was placed on the principle that the EMH debate falls absolutely into the domain of statistical research, and that any attempt to reach a conclusion on the strength of personal observations of market behaviour is fraught with danger. It is natural, however, for investors who are unfamiliar with the research literature to attempt to rationalise their beliefs from their personal experience and this has been shown to offer ample scope for favouring the illusion of inefficiency.

4. *Efficiency applies only to certain shares*

> 'We spend our time looking at stocks which are not covered by a lot of analysts, so that the price is not set by the 'efficient' process. Most Acorn portfolio stocks will be in the 'inefficient' market.'[7]

There are no empirical grounds for believing that a particular group of shares, whether classified by size of company or by any other characteristic, is systematically less efficiently priced than the rest of the market. Indeed, if it could be demonstrated that an inefficient market exists alongside the efficient market, several more funds in addition to Acorn would undoubtedly focus their attention on the former, and as a result, be capable of generating better than average results. However, no evidence for this is available. But there are good reasons why investors might believe that such a submarket exists.

Firstly, a number of investment institutions tend to hold only the shares of large companies, in keeping with the significant amounts of capital that they have to invest. This suggests that some smaller companies will be consistently overlooked by many investment managers, and as a consequence, may be less thoroughly analysed and more susceptible to mispricing. Such a fear, of course, presupposes that the correctness of a price is a direct function of the quantity of analysis carried out, and that the amount of analysis needed to create efficient prices can be measured. However, apart from the fact that large companies may currently be subject to over-analysis, and that smaller companies may require less analysis, there is in practice no way of knowing whether a given input of analysis is insufficient to establish a correct price, except by demonstrating that investors can earn superior returns by trading in the sections of the market alleged to be inadequately analysed.

The second reason why smaller companies might be thought to be less efficiently priced is that it is amongst their shares rather than those of large, well established companies that the illusions of inefficiency are more likely to manifest themselves. The sizeable price movements and sudden reversals of fortune that are more characteristic of relatively small, undiversified companies tend to give credence to the notion that genuine and significant opportunities for abnormal gain are available to the shrewd investor. The fact is, of course, that the more dramatic price movements of smaller companies' shares are perfectly consistent with pricing efficiency, being no more than expressions of their inherently greater volatility. Whatever opportunities these price patterns appear to offer in the light of retrospective analysis, if the prices fully reflect the subsequent chances of loss no less than the chances of gain, they cannot be regarded as any less efficiently set than others.

Finally, suspicion that the shares of smaller firms might be priced on a different basis from leading shares is given further support by a number of empirical studies, some of which were noted in Chapter 5, suggesting that small firms' shares earn higher average returns than those of larger firms.[8] However, it has been argued by one writer[9] that this size anomaly can be substantially attributed to a failure of conventional research methodology to incorporate the effects of infrequent trading, a characteristic of small firms' shares which, if overlooked, can seriously understate their relative riskiness. In effect, the shares of small firms are significantly more risky than they are normally represented, and their apparent superior performance may be entirely the result of mismeasurement.

In conclusion, it is one thing to argue that amongst the thousands of shares that make up the market, there may at any given point in time be some which happen to be mispriced, offering opportunities to those who are able to identify them; it is another, and less credible assertion that there is an identifiable section of the market which is consistently less efficiently priced than the remainder, making the task of the bargain-hunter that much easier to accomplish.

5. Statistical evidence is insufficient

'It is dangerous to rely on extensive statistical analysis without the detailed insight and corroboration of numerous individual examples.'[10]

In Chapter 2 it was shown not to be possible from even the very closest scrutiny of a company's economic circumstances to ascertain unequivocally whether its current share price captures all publicly available and relevant information in an unbiased manner. It always remains too easy for an investor who believes the market to be inefficient to offer apparently sound reasons why the price is wrong, just as it is easy for an investor who believes the contrary to rationalise the price. Hence the need for the detached approach of statistical methods.

The claim above, however, is that the statistical evidence needs the corroboration of individual examples before its findings can be properly evaluated. It should be stressed, of course, that statistical research itself is nothing other than the 'corroboration of numerous examples' where the number included is sufficiently large to eliminate bias and the deceptions of chance. A detailed analysis of specific case studies, however, is as likely to produce a biased impression of events unless one fully comprehends the total information set from which a specific share price on a particular day is derived, as it is to provide a 'detailed insight' into the validity of the price.

Certainly, if statistical research were to establish beyond reasonable doubt the existence of a specific inefficiency, then, of course it would make sense for an investor to analyse individual cases for the purposes of effectively exploiting the inefficiency. But that is a quite different matter from the process of establishing the existence of the inefficiency in the first place. Not only is the statistical approach necessary for that purpose, but it is almost certainly the only useful approach.

A detailed analysis of individual cases may, of course, be useful, and even necessary, to corroborate the validity of the samples used in a specific statistical study, but, once again, this is not the same as providing insights that can be used either to refute or to corroborate the actual findings of the research.

6. *Prices are determined by supply and demand*

'EMH ignores the more obvious issues of supply and demand. These in turn are affected by stock market expectations of likely future returns on shares. And expectations about the future are themselves a function of the state of uncertainty or confidence at the time of measurement of prices.'[11]

If this argument were to be accepted literally, the implication would be that no market of any kind could possibly be efficient, since by definition every market depends on a supply and demand for its product. 'Supply and demand' is merely a description of the mechanism through which security prices are determined. Whether the mechanism is efficient or not cannot be ascertained from the terms used to describe its operation.

The argument presumably envisages the possibility that a holder of a large number of shares may decide, for whatever reason, to sell his holding and that if the demand by buyers does not at the time happen to match the new supply, the price will fall without there necessarily being any change in the underlying worth. If this does occur, then certainly it can be concluded that the forces of supply and demand operate to produce a mechanism that is indeed inefficient, and that shrewd investors should be able to take advantage of the consequences. But to assume that the forces of supply and demand will necessarily operate in this manner is to prejudge the issue. It is no less possible that a downward movement in the price of a security will, if unwarranted by economic conditions, *create* a demand for the security amongst perceptive investors, a demand that may lead to a rapid restoration of the price to its equilibrium level.

It is of course correct to say that supply and demand will be affected by expectations of the future, and that these expectations will be subject to uncertainty. It has never been argued that the market can eliminate uncertainty or that prices can be determined without formulating expectations of the future. The issue is whether the consensus view of the future and the market's ability to cope with uncertainties are more efficient than the efforts of individual investors.

In summary, the assertion that market prices are a product of supply and demand is simply a definitional statement and brings us no closer to determining whether the resulting set of prices does or does not fail to represent the semi-strong worth of the underlying securities.

7. *Whilst there may be little scope in the long term for achieving above average profits, there will always be occasional short-term opportunities*

There are two possible interpretations to this argument:

(a) investors' performances will average out in the long term, but in the short term individual opportunities for abnormal profit may arise, or

(b) no systematic opportunities for abnormal gain will persist over the long term, but investors may periodically be able to profit from special situations or short-term price aberrations.

The first interpretation makes little sense. The long term is nothing other than the aggregate of a succession of short terms, and it is not possible for an investor systematically to make significant gains in the short term without these reflecting themselves in his long-term performance.

The second interpretation is that the opportunities for exceptional profit will not persist over the long term and that any special situations that do occur will be short-lived. This argument certainly recognises an important principle of market efficiency, namely that a competitive market is unlikely to allow any systematic inefficiency to survive for long, and that if opportunities for abnormal profit do arise, it is only because the market has over- or under-reacted in a particular situation.

This does not appear to be an unreasonable speculation, but two points should be considered. Firstly, individual special situations or price aberrations are very difficult to verify at the time, because of the problems of differentiating between chance and good judgment in the interpretation of the events. It is necessary to emphasise once again that when an investor claims to have the good judgment to perceive a special opportunity, he can only formulate that judgment from his own limited set of data, which, unless he has access to privileged information, is by definition almost certainly less complete than the market's. Given this information gap, it is no less likely that what appears in his judgment to be a price aberration is actually the market's correct reaction to information that he does not possess or has misinterpreted. Secondly, if there exist periodic short-term opportunities of significant frequency and magnitude, one would expect investors who have the skill to perceive them to earn a higher than average return over the long term. But this expectation is not supported by the studies of expertly managed funds reported in Chapter 4.

This argument, therefore, highlights a very significant aspect of the debate. Long-term systematic inefficiencies offer real opportunities for exploitable gain, but are unlikely to exist in a highly competitive market; short-term, non-systematic inefficiencies arising out of 'special situations', if they exist at all, are exceedingly difficult to establish before it becomes too late for them to be profitably exploited.

8. *But it is still possible for some investors, such as Keynes, to make a lot of money in the market*

> 'Although the cost of dealing in the market is considerable, a number of investors who deal in shares rather than hold them for a long term do outperform the market.'[12]

There is a natural impulse to assume that any investor who is manifestly outstanding in economic and financial matters should be able to use his comparative advantage to outperform significantly the average, 'financially illiterate' investor. And when such an outstanding individual is actually observed to make money on the market, there is no less an impulse to hold the example up as striking testimony of the market's inability to process information with the same degree of expertise. An example of such an investor is, of course, John Maynard Keynes, whose alleged success in the market is still cited as evidence of the market's potential rewards for the perceptive investor. It is curious, perhaps, that the activities of a single individual, albeit such a prominent one, 50 years ago, should be advanced as evidence of market conditions today.

In Chapter 2, the point was emphasised that, whilst at any given point of time, many investors can technically claim to be currently outperforming the market, roughly as many will be underperforming it. The real issue is whether the former are doing so by chance or by skill. If the above-average performers are consistently professional investors, then this indeed would suggest that the market is inefficient in setting the odds. But the evidence indicates the contrary, that over the long term, the performance of neither skilled nor naive investors will systematically deviate from the average to any significant extent. And it is the results over the long term that are significant.

When someone of Keynes' stature is reputed to have been on the winning side, it seems to be regarded as unworthy to suggest the possibility that he, like others, may have enjoyed a run of good luck. His reputation is based largely on the fact that, during his office as Chairman of the National Mutual Life Assurance Society, he increased their profits substantially, and that he also personally amassed considerable wealth after the stock market crash of 1929. But, against these facts, a number of others are also worthy of note:[13]

(a) Because of his prominence in public affairs, and his acknowledged expertise in matters such as the money system and interest rates, Keynes was able, through his speeches, to influence events, and this in a sense, arguably placed him in the position of being a market insider.

(b) A material part of his success in the National Mutual may have been attributable to the fact that he persuaded the society to change their investment policy from holding predominantly fixed interest stocks to a substantial investment in equities. This change of policy could be expected in the normal course of events to produce a higher level of profits.

(c) In 1930 he was removed from office as Chairman of the Independent Investment Trust because, under his leadership, the fund had virtually lost its entire capital.

In conclusion, we do not have enough evidence to determine whether Keynes' investment performance was the product of insight or of chance, an uncertainty that generally holds inevitably for any single individual investor's performance. The fact that he was able to remark in his early years: 'I would have thought that the right investment policy for the National Mutual would be to hold one security only and change it every week at the board meeting',[14] certainly suggests more of the confident speculator than the mature investor. The fact that 'in the end he began to get disillusioned with an active investment policy . . . and to believe that it was wise to concentrate on long-term equity holdings',[15] suggests a growing awareness of the symptoms of market efficiency.

9. What about Joseph Granville?

On two separate occasions during 1981 the American analyst, Joseph Granville, was associated with a dramatic and sudden collapse of the securities market. In January 1981, he issued a 'sell-everything' order to his clients and within the day the Dow Jones Industrial Average fell 31 points. On 23 September, he offered similar advice on an early morning radio programme in London, and the UK market experienced on the same day its second greatest fall on record, with the FT Index going down more than 20 points. He followed this with a prediction that on the following Monday, 28 September, there would be a fall in Wall Street that would earn a page in financial history. Within an hour of its opening on the Monday, the UK market had fallen by 23 points, the greatest fall ever in such a short period, to finish 17 points down on the day. Wall Street, which is of course several hours behind London, started with a sharp decline of 13 points, but turned about to finish 18 points *up* on the day. On Tuesday, Wall Street prices rose again and the UK market recovered all of its previous day's fall. Finally, in addition to these short-term events, Granville at the same time forecast that during the year 1981–2 the US and UK markets would decline to their 1974 levels (although he is reported to have retreated a little when he was reminded that the FT Index had been as low as 150 in 1974 compared to the then current price of around 500).

These incidents have tended to be interpreted as evidence of gross inefficiency on the part of the market and of a general herd instinct amongst investors. Their significance, therefore, deserves to be examined, particularly since they provide a useful illustration of some important principles established in earlier chapters. It should be emphasised, however, that the writer has no data relating to Granville other than that published in the financial press.

The explanation which Granville himself offered for the various events is that, on the basis of his technical analysis, he successfully predicted the falls, and that his lack of success on the Monday was due to a combination of misfortune and a concerted effort by Wall Street specialists to defeat him. Some alternative explanations, however, are possible:

(a)   *The entire series of events may have been due to chance.* If one were to plot the apparent successes of all analysts, then it is perfectly compatible with market efficiency that by chance a few analysts would periodically produce an impressive series of good predictions. It may be that research will reveal that Granville's predictive powers are beyond the realms of chance, but until proof is forthcoming, the possibility that his reputation is substantially due to good fortune cannot be ruled out. Indeed, on the day after he issued his 'Blue Monday' prediction a leading London analyst from Phillips and Drew declared that shares were now cheap and forecast a rise. Was it he rather than Granville that had the predictive power that day, and if so, how is one to discriminate between the two before the event? If Granville's performance is to be distinguished from chance, it has to pass the same rigorous tests that were earlier described as the accepted benchmark for establishing any exploitable inefficiency.

(b)   *What appeared to be a prediction might simply have been due to good timing in reporting the present.* It could be argued that the proximity of Granville's pronouncements to the subsequent occurrences implied that he was doing little more than reporting the present, rather than predicting the future. The dramatic fall in London that followed upon his early morning radio programme might have been expected by many observers to have taken place in response to a fall that had preceded it on Wall Street some hours before. There were also arguably many other sound economic reasons why the market might have declined—sharply rising interest rates, a falling pound, concern about the adequacy of President Reagan's recently announced counter-inflation policies. It is possible that Granville combined an acute sensitivity to what was actually happening with remarkable publicity acumen, and that during the period in question, he merely observed and verbalised the market's traumatic short-term adjustment to changing events.

(c)   *He may have caused the fall.* Although the Chairman of the London Stock Exchange at the time denied that Granville caused the fall, there is little doubt that this is the interpretation placed on the events by several commentators. But how could it be possible for the views of a single analyst to influence not just the New York and London markets but possibly several of the world's markets?

(i)   If he has a sufficient number of influential followers, it is conceivable that Granville could temporarily affect the aggregate supply–demand relationship for investment funds, and as a result, marginally affect the current price of risk capital.

(ii) Because of his reputation, whether deserved or not, the market might take account of the possibility that Granville's pronouncements could exert influence in the short term on the strategies adopted by key businessmen and politicians and, as a result, help delay the implementation of anti-recessionary policies. It may be viewed as irrational for businessmen or politicians to place any significant weight on his statements, but it is not irrational for the market to take account of the possibility that they might do so.

(iii) Granville might have been recognised by the market as a potential source of additional information under conditions of severe uncertainty. If the view were taken that his past record was sufficient to make it possible that he possessed a unique interpretative insight into future economic events, then it would be quite rational for the market to take at least some account of what he said in its pricing decisions. The existence of an individual with superior insight is quite consistent with the concept of near efficiency, because, given the rarity of the phenomenon and the fact that the market responded virtually instantaneously, the event does not appear to constitute a serious inefficiency capable of being exploited by investors.

The falls, of course, could have been due to a combination of all three factors. It is simply not possible to reach a satisfactory verdict without more data. But it is a reasonable conclusion, in the meantime, that despite the dramatic quality of the events, they are not sufficient in themselves to undermine confidence in the market's efficiency generally or to warrant active discipleship of Granville in particular.

The episode, however, does provide two important lessons for the efficient market debate:

(a) It highlights the strong illusion of inefficiency that can be created by a well-known market personality whose achievements might simply be due entirely to a combination of good fortune and engineered publicity exploits. This is not to say for certain that Granville can be dismissed on these grounds, but it should alert us to the need for constant vigilance against being diverted by such isolated phenomena from the general findings of the research literature.

(b) It underlines the danger to investors when an individual earns such a reputation and the confidence that goes with it. Presumably because Granville truly believed that Blue Monday would occur, whether predicted or caused by him, he issued the advice generally, 'even to eighty year old grandmothers', to sell short. This indeed is risky advice, since, theoretically at least, the potential loss in selling short is virtually unlimited.

The Implications of Efficiency

If the nature of efficiency is misunderstood, then it is all the more likely that its implications will be incorrectly assessed. A number of arguments rejecting the concept are based essentially on misconceptions of the logical consequences of efficiency:

10. EMH implies that one share is as good as any other

'How many investors could be persuaded to entrust the fate of their capital to the throw of a dart, to a blind belief that at any given moment a security sells at a fair price?'[16]

The significance of the empirical findings is that for the purposes of obtaining an *abnormally* high rate of return, one share has by and large as good a chance as any other. 'Throwing a dart', for most investors, is likely to be as successful a method of identifying mispriced securities as the analysis of publicly available data. But this does not imply that throwing a dart *per se* is a desirable basis for selecting investments. The management of risk remains a fundamental and necessary component of investment strategy, even in an efficient market, and, as will be shown in the next chapter, this may call for considerable care and analysis.

A similar misunderstanding is that EMH implies that one company is as good as any other, a view that is patently untrue. It is obvious, even from casual observation, that certain industries thrive at times when others decline, and that within an industry, certain companies are better managed than their competitors. Efficient market theory does not deny these basic facts. It does, however, distinguish between the company and its stock. The shares of a well-managed company in a growth industry are not necessarily any more desirable than the shares of a less well-managed company in a declining industry, provided the prices of the respective shares fully discount the different circumstances of the two companies. The former may be expected to achieve a higher return from the operation of its productive assets, but if the price of its shares fully reflects this expectation, then a purchaser of the shares will have no better prospect of obtaining an abnormally high return than he would by buying the shares of the latter.

11. An efficient market should not fluctuate so extensively

'Disney fell 86% between 1972 and 1974, with its P/E ratio declining from 64 to 21, though earnings and profit margins improved throughout this period. When was the market efficient? When it took Disney up to 119⅛ or when it put it back to 16⅝? Obviously, perfectly efficient markets should not exhibit such behaviour.'[17]

This is not dissimilar from the problem of speculative bubbles discussed under section 3, except that there the issue was how to reconcile market efficiency with dramatic price movements associated with information signals of dubious quality. Here, the problem is simply to explain how a share can have several markedly different prices within a relatively short period of time and be efficiently priced in each case.

Without considering the specific circumstances of Disney during 1972–4, if one accepts the possibility that the outlook and circumstances of a particular company can change dramatically during a relatively short time period, then one must accept that not only is it possible periodically for prices to fluctuate considerably in an efficient market, but it may be essential. The market's pricing efficiency implies a capacity to respond to any relevant economic information about firms made available to it. It says nothing about the stability of such firms' economic circumstances. If the underlying conditions of a company alter dramatically over short periods of time, an efficient reaction on the part of the market must necessarily lead to correspondingly dramatic movements in the share price. It is begging the question for the above writer to imply that the decline in Disney's stock to 21, 'though earnings and profit margins improved throughout the period', is an indication of efficiency. A P/E of 64 suggests that the market expected a significant improvement in profits. If that expectation was reasonable, given the economic prospects at the time, then it is right that the shares should have subsequently declined when it became clear that the improvement in earnings and profit margins was lower than expected.

12. *Investors would lose interest if the market were efficient*

> 'For investors, the efficient market seems a little like Mark Twain's impish description of heaven, where a person, as a reward, would sit piously with his fellows, singing hymns through eternity, denied all the earthly frivolity that gives life its sparkle.'[18]

The assumption here is that investment is a form of game where the object is to beat-the-market, and that if this cannot be accomplished by the skill of the player, the game will lose its interest. But this ignores the fact that, as with any market, a commodity is being traded, and that it is to the advantage of most participators that the market be price-efficient, so that the commodity can be bought and sold in the knowledge that the price is a fair one, without having to incur the cost or effort of looking behind the price. It will be argued in the next chapter that the primary object of investing in securities is not to beat the market, but to acquire assets that provide future returns commensurate with risk. The mass of investors are no more likely to be deterred from purchasing securities as a result of discovering that the securities market is efficient, than the buyers of antiques would be if the antiques market were found to be comparably efficient. As for the speculators who demand 'earthly frivolity', even an efficient market can still be attractive to them. Efficiency implies that an excess return can be achieved only by chance, but, nonetheless, it can be achieved by chance, and if the speculator decides to 'bet' on an individual share, rather than to buy a diversified portfolio, he obtains the chance of earning a significant excess return, just as he has a chance of suffering a significant loss. But the *ex ante* expected return of this gamble is positive, because correctly priced shares can of course be expected on average to earn a positive return. The same cannot be said of the expected return at the roulette table or the race track.

It must also be stressed that the buy-and-hold-the-market strategy predicated by efficient market theory does not restrict investors to a low risk policy. The object of such a strategy is simply to rid the investor of all *diversifiable* risk, but it can still accommodate the tastes of the investor with the very highest risk preferences. Chapter 7 will demonstrate that, even holding the market, he can attain as high a risk posture through borrowing, as any single-security speculator, except that the former will always have a significantly better expected reward-to-risk ratio.

13. *If the market were efficient, experts should know it*

'The thousands of intelligent analysts are assumed to be capable enough to keep our security market efficient through their efforts but are not intelligent enough to realise that their efforts can yield no individual advantage.'[19]

This comment fails to recognise the enormous difficulty involved in distinguishing between results that are due to chance and those that are due to systematic skill. It is not a question of intelligence. No single individual's experience could amount to a statistically significant sample from which to draw valid conclusions, although no doubt even experts find it difficult to prevent their beliefs being influenced substantially by those experiences. In Chapter 3, it was argued that investment experiences by their nature tend to consist of events that create the illusion of market inefficiency, and it is understandable that many analysts might be victims of the same illusion and fail to give serious consideration to the possibility that the market is efficient, and that much of their apparent personal success is due to chance.

It is for these reasons that researchers include in their analyses significantly lengthy periods of time, large numbers of transactions, and sophisticated adjustments for risk differentials. It would be unreasonable to expect even expert analysts to be able individually to perform the same degree of rigorous analysis undertaken by professional researchers. Moreover, even when presented with the empirical evidence, it requires considerable persuasion to acknowledge that what were hitherto viewed as successful investment decisions might have been no more than the product of good fortune.

It is, however, misleading to suggest that no experts ever learn through their own experience to recognise the signs of the market's pricing efficiency. Benjamin Graham, the pioneer of fundamental research in the 1930s and co-author of what has been for generations a leading textbook of security analysis, observed towards the end of his life:

> 'I am no longer an advocate of elaborate techniques of security analysis in order to find superior value opportunities. This was a rewarding activity, say 40 years ago, when our textbook "Graham and Dodd" was first published; but the situation has changed a good deal since then ... In the light of the enormous amount of research now being carried on, I doubt whether in most cases such extensive efforts will generate sufficiently superior selections to justify their cost. To that very limited extent, I'm on the side of the "efficient market" school of thought now generally accepted by the professors'.[20]

14.   The market would cease to be efficient if everyone believed in EMH

> 'There is a curious paradox. In order for the hypothesis to be true, it is necessary for many investors to disbelieve it. That is, market prices will promptly and fully reflect what is knowable about the companies whose shares are traded only if investors seek to earn superior returns ... If that effort were abandoned, the efficiency of the market would diminish rapidly.'[21]

It is misleading to suggest that a rejection of EMH is a necessary condition for efficiency either to be achieved or sustained. It needs to be stressed again that, for the market to be efficient for practical investment purposes, it does not need to be perfectly efficient in the sense of prices being correct to the penny. The market can be viewed as near efficient if its degree of efficiency is enough for it to serve the interests of the great majority of investors to pursue the passive, least-cost strategy of efficient market theory, even if it is insufficient to prevent highly skilled professional investors from earning an economic rent from their trading activities. In this sense, it is quite conceivable for all investors to believe that the market is efficient without it thereby ceasing to be so. If there is any paradox, it is that the market is probably incapable of being *perfectly* efficient unless some experts disbelieve it or, alternatively, unless some experts are remunerated by some means or other for performing their information-processing function.

One of the more serious aspects of this allegation is that it suggests that it could be desirable for the research findings favouring efficiency not to be widely disseminated. But, in practice, it must assuredly be beneficial for participants in an efficient market to know that it is efficient. Firstly, analysts can be alerted to the possibility that at least some of their analytical activity may be futile and unnecessary. There is no way of knowing precisely, of course, what quantity of information-processing activity is necessary to make the market efficient, but it is possible that even if the collective effect of investors' use of information is to produce a near perfect pricing mechanism, a number of individual investors' use of information may be inefficient or superfluous. This ineffectual activity[22] may be more readily recognised with greater awareness of the evidence.

Secondly, the ordinary investor can also benefit from an awareness of the market's efficiency. One of the more important implications of near efficiency is that the ordinary investor is not only unable personally to outperform the market, but is unable to profit from the superior insights of the expert minority, because any attempt by the latter to transmit investment advice will reflect itself in the share price. But this effect will not necessarily be evident to ordinary investors who, in ignorance, may be diverted from the more profitable passive strategy unless the evidence favouring efficiency is effectively communicated to them.

Conclusion

It is not suggested that everyone who supports the conventional view would necessarily employ any one or more of the preceding arguments in its defence. It is a fact, however, that countless investors do subscribe to the conventional view, and it is a fair assumption that few are personally familiar with the empirical research literature. Therefore, the majority must base their stance on arguments of the kind. The list, undoubtedly, is not exhaustive. Others could have been added that perhaps are little more than variations of one or more of those presented. For example, 'EMH ignores market psychology',[23] is essentially a composite of sections 2, 3 and 6. 'It cannot be good to diversify widely—you can't beat the market that way'[24] is a variation of 12 and will be picked up again in the next chapter. There are undoubtedly others which should have been included but which were overlooked by the author. But if three principles are recognised, it becomes a relatively straightforward matter to differentiate between the spurious assertion and the truly valid criticism of EMH:

(a) EMH makes no assumptions about the process by which the market becomes efficient.
(b) Efficiency is purely an empirical issue, testable only by rigorous statistical analysis.
(c) The visible characteristics of the market as it is today are quite consistent with market efficiency.

Notes and References

1. Dreman, D. (1977) *Psychology and the Stock Market*, Amocom, p. 237.
2. Dreman, *ibid.* p. 220.
3. Dreman, *ibid.* p. 243.
4. For example, see Beaver, W. (1981) *Financial Reporting: An Accounting Revolution*, Prentice-Hall, p. 160.
5. Bethlehem, R.W. (1979) 'Reservations concerning the efficient market hypothesis', *Investment Analyst*, September.
6. Some of the more celebrated 'speculative bubbles' have in fact been in the Australian mining sector. Poseidon shares, for example, in 1969 rose in a matter of weeks from $1.22 to $190, and subsequently fell back to $1. However, the events that follow are imaginary and for illustrative purposes.
7. *First Quarter Report*, Acorn Fund (1976), 31 March.
8. For example, see Reinganum, M.R. (1981b) 'Misspecification of capital asset pricing: empirical anomalies based on earnings' yields and market values', *Journal of Financial Economics*, 9, March.
9. Roll, R. (1981) 'A possible explanation of the small firm effect', *Journal of Finance*, September.
10. Dreman, D. *op. cit.* p. 42.
11. Kusseff, S. (1981) book review in *Accountancy Age*, 12 January.
12. Kusseff, S. *ibid.*
13. Davenport, N. (1975) 'Keynes in the city', in *Essays on John Maynard Keynes*, ed. M. Keynes, Cambridge University Press, p. 227.
14. Davenport, *ibid.* p. 225.
15. Davenport, *ibid.* pp. 228–9.
16. Bernstein, L.A. (1975) 'In defense of fundamental analysis', *Financial Analysts Journal*, January/February, p. 59.
17. Dreman, D. *op. cit.* p. 54.
18. Dreman, D. (1978) 'Don't go with the pros', *Barron's*, May 8, p. 11.
19. Bernstein, L.A. (1978) *Financial Statement Analysis*, Irwin, p. 54.

20. 'A conversation with Benjamin Graham', *Financial Analysts Journal*, September/October, 1976.
21. Lorie, J. and Hamilton, M. (1973) *The Stock Market: Theories and Evidence*, Irwin, p. 98.
22. See, for example, Hirshleifer, J. and Riley, J. (1979) 'The analytics of uncertainty and information, an expository survey', *Journal of Economic Literature*, December, pp. 1404–6.
23. Dreman, *op. cit. passim.*
24. For example, see Belfer, N. (1965) 'Determining the construction of an individual securities portfolio', *Financial Analysts Journal*, May/June.

7

The Implications for Investors and Investment Advisers

It has been stressed in earlier chapters that the significance of market efficiency lies in its practical consequences for stock market participants. It is not possible to appreciate this signifcance, nor to recognise the costs associated with conventional investment behaviour, unless the behaviour appropriate to efficient market conditions is fully specified. The purpose of this chapter is to present the logical consequences for investors and investment advisers if conditions of near efficiency are assumed to operate.

Investors

The primary motivation for investors is assumed to be to secure a return commensurate with risk. But for anyone who perceives the market to be inefficient, a secondary goal may exist, namely to exceed the average rate needed to compensate for risk, in effect to outperform the market. For some investors this secondary goal could even become the dominant motive and significantly influence their investment strategy.

For the sake of illustration, assume that a particular investor's motives are completely dominated by the drive to earn excess returns, and that all else is subservient to beating the market. His position is analogous to that of a participator in an investment game where the object is simply to win. Clearly, under such circumstances, it is not desirable to hold the market, because by definition, this would make it impossible for the investor to beat the market. At the limit, he should hold the one single security which he believes to be the most underpriced, since the extent to which he engages in any diversification, the nearer will his subsequent performance duplicate that of the market. By so doing, he is maximising his chances of achieving a superior return, although, at the same time, increasing his chances of achieving an inferior return.

In practice, few investors are likely to hold such an extreme position as to be motivated solely by the desire to beat the market. Their goal will be a mixture of the primary desire to achieve the going return for the risk assumed and the desire to do better than average. If market prices are determined after taking account of investors' ability to diversify a certain proportion of risk away, then the investor is unlikely to achieve his primary goal without some degree of diversification. But the more diversified he becomes, the more he diminishes the chance of achieving his secondary goal. The two goals are in sharp conflict. This conflict is recognised explicitly by several writers,[1] although perhaps nowhere more poignantly than in the legendary advice of Andrew Carnegie that the secret to amassing wealth is 'to put all one's eggs in one basket and to watch the basket'.

The other extreme is that implied by efficient market theory. The secondary motive ceases to have any rational significance for the risk-averse investor in a world where shares are so efficiently priced that the market can be beaten only by good fortune. It is this world that we are concerned with here.

The Theoretically Ideal Solution

The traditional emphasis on the search for mispriced securities has tended to inhibit the development of an optimal solution to the primary goal of investment, in particular, with respect to the investor's control of risk. Figures 7.1 to 7.3 illustrate three key concepts which highlight the distinction between traditional investment philosophy and the insights of modern investment theory.

(1) *According to conventional theory, a different portfolio should be constructed to suit the risk preferences of each individual investor.*

Figure 7.1 reflects the conventional approach to satisfying the needs of individual investors. *B* represents a riskless government bond. *L*, *M* and *H* represent respectively three risky portfolios each with progressively greater returns to compensate for the increasing risks. *L* is a portfolio comprising blue-chip, low-risk securities, *M* a portfolio of medium risk and *H* a portfolio comprising only high-risk, high-return securities. Setting aside the possibility of constructing a portfolio composed of undervalued securities, the traditional investment philosophy consists of directing the investor to the portfolio that best suits his particular risk preference. The investor who wishes to avoid all risk will invest his entire funds in *B*. The investor who is prepared to bear some risk for a higher return will chose a low, medium or high-risk portfolio according to his individual preference.

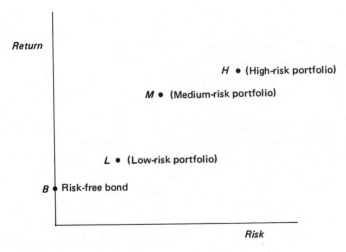

Figure 7.1

(2) *A broadly diversified portfolio such as M offers a higher return per
unit of risk than either a low or high-risk portfolio.*

In Figure 7.1, for simplicity, only three possible risky portfolios were
envisaged. Figure 7.2 reflects the reality that, by varying the ratio and
character of the component securities, an infinite number of efficient
portfolios can be constructed on the curve *LH*. Since a north-westerly
direction on the graph is more desirable than any other, then there exists
a point *M* on the curve *LH* which has a higher relative return for its risk
content than any other. The reason for this is that, to construct, say,
portfolio *L* or *H*, only a relatively few securities may be available in the
respective risk categories. Portfolio *M*, on the other hand, can be constructed by including not only all available medium-risk securities, but
also the extreme securities that comprise portfolios *L* and *H*. The diversification effect is, therefore, more pronounced in *M* than in any other
combination.

(3) *According to modern investment theory, the superior risk-reward payoff
of a broadly diversified portfolio can be exploited by all investors
irrespective of their personal risk preferences.*

It is this simple observation that has revolutionised investment theory.
When presented with the range of alternatives offered in Figure 7.2, the
conventional advice to the investor is to select the point on curve *LH* that
best suits his individual taste. Whilst recognising that *M* is in one sense a
best-buy, the investor who seeks only a low-risk posture is nonetheless
directed to a portfolio of low-risk securities at a point near *L*, and the
more aggressive investor to a portfolio at a point near *H*. The investor
whose tastes happen to coincide with *M* is regarded simply as fortunate
that he should obtain the best available reward-to-risk ratio.

The main insight of modern capital market theory[2] is that this best-
buy property of *M* can be taken advantage of by everyone, whatever their
tastes. The appropriate strategy is depicted in Figure 7.3 where a line
has been drawn from *B* through *M*. The significance of the line is that an
investor can view his investment opportunities as consisting of only two
assets, the risky portfolio *M* and the riskless security *B*. By apportioning
his funds between the two, the investor is able to achieve any risk-return
position he desires on the line *BM*. It is apparent that whatever point he
selects, the result dominates any corresponding point on the curve *LH* in
the sense that it offers a higher return for a given level of risk or lower
risk for a given level of return. The dotted line represents the strategy of

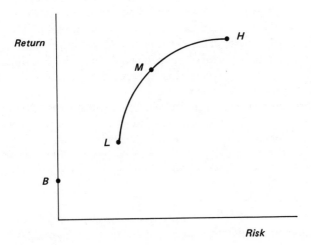

Figure 7.2

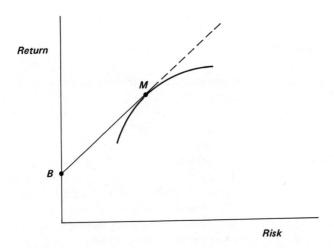

Figure 7.3

the aggressive investor who previously would have been advised to buy portfolio H. This time, instead of buying debt capital (investing in B), he becomes an issuer of debt (that is, he borrows) and invests in M. As a result, he not only invests all his own capital in M but the proceeds of his borrowings. He can thus achieve any point on the extended line through M and such a strategy will secure a higher return per unit of risk than any corresponding point near H on the curve LH.

Therefore, although the theoretical solution might appear at first sight to be insensitive to individual investors' tastes, insofar as it recommends the same portfolio of risky assets for all investors alike, all tastes are in fact accommodated through the accompanying process of borrowing or lending, which allows greater or lesser commitment to the risky portfolio.

What is M?

M is the most efficiently diversified portfolio available, a portfolio comprising all risky assets in the market in their value-weighted proportions. How can we know that the line drawn from B tangent to the curve will happen to pass through the 'market portfolio' M? If M did not include every marketable risky asset, the implication would be that certain assets are not worth holding. But if the market is efficient, every security in it will be priced so that it offers the return appropriate for its level of risk, and will, therefore, be worth holding. Hence, M must include all marketable assets.

The Market Portfolio

The solutions of both theory and practice, therefore, depend significantly on the concept of a market portfolio. In the context, however, providing a precise definition of the market is not without difficulty. Researchers frequently tend for convenience to treat the market as being synonymous with the national securities market, the New York or UK Stock Exchanges, etc. But theory implies that the market portfolio should comprise *all* risky assets. To the extent that private residences, antiques, works of art etc. can properly be viewed as investments, then these, presumably, must also be viewed as valid components of the market portfolio. In addition, all corporate bonds are included, contradicting the generally accepted presumption that a bond-holder is a distinct class of investor from the equity-holder. More importantly, however, the

Table 7.1 *Market Value of Equities Expressed as Percentage of World Market*

USA	45%
Japan	18%
UK	7%
Other European Countries	16%
Canada	6%
Australia	1%
Others	7%

Source: Stock Exchange Fact Book, March 1979

market portfolio is not restricted to the assets of the investor's home country. It is essentially a world market since it is now recognised that international diversification yields significant risk-reducing benefits.[3] The approximate national components of the world portfolio are shown in Table 7.1. If one assumes that all leading stock markets have efficient pricing mechanisms and that they are sufficiently integrated to produce a common risk-reward relationship, then the investor's portfolio should logically consist as far as possible of these proportions. With the possible exception of residents of the United States, the investor's holding of domestic securities should therefore form only a minor proportion of his portfolio, with the nationals of small countries such as Australia holding as much as 99% foreign securities.

Of course, the corollary of this rule is that the major portion of the equity capital of virtually every country in the world will be held by non-nationals. The price that has to be paid by a country for reducing the cost of its risk capital is, therefore, to accept a dominantly foreign ownership of its listed securities. Market efficiency, it seems, has potentially far-reaching political implications.

The Solution in Practice

The solution in practice differs from the purely theoretical solution primarily because of transaction costs and, to a lesser extent, taxation. But the differences are not enough to convert a passive strategy into an active one—they simply necessitate some degree of tailoring in the selection and management of the risky portfolio.

In the first place, it is not practicable for an individual investor literally to acquire the market portfolio. There are too many components for it to be economically feasible for most investors to allocate their capital amongst every marketable security available. It can be shown, however, that 90% of diversifiable risk can be eliminated with only about 20 securities.[4] Therefore, the first difference from the theoretical solution is that the portfolio held by the investor will be a proxy portfolio, a microcosm of the total market.

The second difference is that it is probably desirable for investors to tailor the selection of securities to suit their personal taxation requirements, low-yielding securities for high tax payers and high-yielding securities for low tax payers.

The third difference is a direct consequence of the previous two. In contrast to the pure buy-and-hold policy of theory, the investor in practice will find it necessary periodically to revise his portfolio: (1) if the relative values of the components change sufficiently to alter the balance of the portfolio; (2) if the risks of the component securities change; and (3) to generate tax losses, or where annual taxation reliefs make it desirable to realise a proportion of any capital gains.[5]

Periodic revision of the portfolio is necessary, therefore, mainly because of the need to ensure that the proxy portfolio continues to match the characteristics of the market. This revision process necessarily involves transaction costs, although it was transaction costs in the first place that necessitated the selection of a surrogate portfolio rather than the market portfolio itself. There is a trade-off between the costs of setting up a portfolio, where the costs are partly a function of how many securities are involved and the costs of revising a portfolio where the frequency of revision is a function of how few securities are involved.

Index Funds

Under efficient market conditions, the individual investor's concern is to secure and maintain efficient diversification with minimum cost. We have seen that there are costs in constructing a portfolio composed of large numbers of securities, but that a portfolio containing only a few securities requires frequent revision, and that too has its costs. Financial institutions, however, have responded to this problem by establishing index funds — funds where the policy is simply to duplicate the market portfolio. Their size makes it possible to purchase at relatively low cost the necessary breadth of selection needed to capture the full diversification effects of the market portfolio, thereby avoiding the need for frequent revision. In addition, the index fund has the advantage over the conventional fund that research costs are virtually zero. Although a minimal amount of management is necessary to prevent the fund from diverging from the market index, the overall costs are low. For example, the managers of the American National Bank's Index Fund estimate that their trading costs are less than 0.02% compared to $1\frac{1}{2}$–3% for the conventional portfolio.[6]

A further advantage of the index fund compared to a personal portfolio is that a fund is better able than individuals to borrow at a more favourable rate of interest in order to create the leveraged position sought by those investors whose preferences are located on the dotted line of Figure 7.3.

Despite their increasing popularity and apparent success, however, index funds have predictably attracted criticism by those who continue to believe that beating the market is a prime object of investment. One commentator observes:

> 'Index funds are a negative approach. The Standard and Poor itself represents two-thirds of the market value of all stocks and so by definition cannot provide above-average results. If you settle for simply matching it, you're throwing in the towel—you're conceding defeat.'[7]

Such a comment illustrates the conflict created by the two basic investment goals and demonstrates why an emphasis on beating the market is antagonistic to efficient diversification. So far from being a matter for criticism, the rationale and merit of the index fund is precisely that it does not produce results that are above or below average. The issue is not whether an index fund is an efficient investment vehicle, but whether there is enough evidence to justify pursuing the alternative policy of active trading and incomplete diversification. If not, the index fund is the logical course for most investors.

The conflict between optimal diversification and beating the market is most clearly evidenced by the strategies adopted by the many orthodox investment institutions which reject the index fund solution. The primary commodity traded by mutual funds and unit trusts etc. is effective diversification, but the basic principles of good diversification are characteristically undermined by the widespread practice of specialising in one sector of the market, such as a particular industrial grouping (e.g. oil and natural resources) or a specific geographical grouping (e.g. Far

Eastern stocks). By so doing, the investment institution restricts the impact of diversification in order to avoid the perceived disadvantage of the index fund being condemned inescapably to an average performance. The possibility of beating the market is left open, but the price to be paid is the possibility of underperforming the market, with its adverse consequences for the reputation of the finance house. Marketing considerations, therefore, have induced many finance houses to operate several such funds simultaneously, each fund focusing on a different sector of the market. The effect is to make the collective investment holding of the finance house substantially equal to the market portfolio, whilst its individual funds remain so diverse that chance alone offers a high probability of at least one fund ranking amongst the high performers in the annual performance league.

It is clear, therefore, that under efficient market conditions, unless the principle is more widely accepted that a successful fund is one which achieves an average performance every year rather than a volatile sequence of above and below average performances, the principles of sound diversification will tend to be the casualty of marketing expediency.

The concept of the index fund, it should be said, is not entirely new. It is perhaps a credit to the good instinct of the managers of the Scottish trusts of the nineteenth century that, instead of attempting to pick winners, they explicitly set out to construct portfolios that reflected the universe of available securities.[8]

If the index funds currently in existence are to be criticised for anything, it is that many are constructed on the assumption that the universe of risky securities is limited to domestic securities. The ideal index fund is one that mirrors the world portfolio.

Individual Risk Preferences

It needs to be stressed again that the index fund solution does not commit all investors to the same degree of risk. The individual establishes his preferred risk-return position by combining his holding in the market portfolio with a borrowing or lending arrangement that enhances or reduces his total risk exposure. The solution, therefore, accommodates equally the most cautious and the most speculative tastes.

The unbroken capital market line *BM* of Figure 7.3, however, assumes that, to achieve this effect, an investor can borrow or lend at the same rate of interest. In reality, this may not be feasible, which suggests

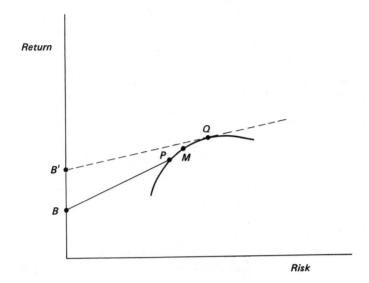

Figure 7.4

the possible need for some modification to the ideal solution. If the two rates are in fact unequal, and the investor has to pay a rate B' for his borrowings, then there will not be one but two lines, as in Figure 7.4, together with two points of tangency to the curve. This implies that the low-risk taker should allocate his capital between the riskless bond B with the risky portfolio P, a portfolio of somewhat lower risk than that of M, whilst the high-risk taker should combine an investment in the slightly more risky portfolio Q with personal borrowing at rate B'. The middle-risk investor would have to select a portfolio on the curve between P and Q which best satisfies his risk preference, and which may of course be slightly more or less risky than M.

But this complication does not necessarily undermine the general validity of the basic model for two reasons:

(a) The relevant borrowing rate for comparison purposes is not the rate an individual would pay personally, but the rate payable by a large, perfectly diversified index fund, because, just as an investor can readily arrange his investment diversification through an intermediary, so he can effect his borrowing. The rate payable by such an institution for its borrowing may well not be materially different from the lending rate. But why, if the market measures risk consistently, should the cost of a loan to an individual intending to use the capital for the purchase of securities cost more than a loan to an institution which uses the capital for the same purpose? The rate of interest charged by a lender depends in part on his perception of the creditworthiness of the borrower. This perception will be based on the information available about the latter. A lender is more likely to be convinced that a well-established index fund will apply the funds for the purchase of an efficiently diversified portfolio than an individual, whatever the intention of the latter. Investment institutions are bound by their charter and obliged to publish financial reports. Therefore, even if the underlying risks are in fact the same in both cases, lenders may charge the individual a premium to compensate for their greater subjective uncertainty about the level of risk. The individual could partly overcome this relative disadvantage by publishing regular financial reports, but it would clearly be informationally more efficient for a group of potential borrowers to proceed under one corporate umbrella than to publish possibly thousands of separate reports.

(b) The significance of the now classic investment solution of Figure 7.3 is not so much that all investors should hold literally the same portfolio as that they should all hold very well-diversified portfolios. Unless there is a material difference between the lending and borrowing rates, the difference in composition between the portfolios lying between P and Q is unlikely to be significant. Indeed, it has become apparent that in practice it is a very difficult task to define M precisely, but what is important is that any portfolio that is even an approximation to the concept of M will capture the essence of the underlying principle. It will certainly be a materially different portfolio from the conventional notion of what constitutes efficient diversification.

Is an Efficient Market Possible if all Investors Hold the Market Portfolio?

Some writers have argued that portfolio theory is incompatible with market efficiency on the grounds that if every investor devoted only a fraction of his portfolio to any one security, the price of the security could not react instantaneously to the new information unless the information reached all investors simultaneously.[9] Strictly, of course, it is the compatibility of the Capital Asset Pricing Model rather than portfolio theory that is being questioned. The latter is concerned with the technology of constructing an efficient portfolio, the former teaches that if the market is perfectly efficient the optimal portfolio for every investor is the market portfolio. The above argument is that, if all investors hold the market portfolio, then each must respond actively to every item of relevant information for the information to reflect itself in the share price. But this is not the case, because if investors follow theory literally, by holding a fraction of every security available, then whatever change takes place in the composition of the market portfolio, the individual portfolios will automatically reflect the market without any action being taken by investors. If new information favourable to one particular security is published, a single transaction should be enough for the new price to manifest itself. Investors would not need to make any adjustment to their portfolios. It is not necessary that the new information reach all investors simultaneously for the price of a share to reach its correct level. It is sufficient that the information reach those investors who happen at the time to be engaged in buying or selling securities.

In practice, of course, investors are likely to make a compromise with the strict principles of portfolio theory by holding no more than a proxy for the market portfolio, composed of a limited number of securities rather than the literal solution of holding a proportion of every share in the market. For any investor that happens now to hold the security in question, then some adjustment to the balance of the portfolio may be required as a result of the change in price, because an increase in value of a single component may cause it no longer to be a good proxy for the market.

In most cases, however, it should not be necessary for investors to respond directly to the new information for the purposes of carrying out this rebalancing process. It is the change in share price resulting from the information and not the information itself that is the relevant signal, and, therefore, most investors can secure an optimal balance on their portfolios without receiving or studying the original information.[10]

Of course the professional traders who set the price in response to the new information may in the process have to set aside the principles of portfolio theory, so, to that extent, market efficiency may in practice appear to be incompatible with portfolio theory. But it is still fair to say that there is no fundamental conflict between the two theories, since the position of the professional trader arises only because investors do not apply the strict portfolio rules of holding a fraction of every security in the market, and because the trader's function is to make up for the informational-processing deficiencies of the ordinary investor. For the general investor, not only is market efficiency compatible with portfolio theory, but the two are quite complementary.

Investment Advisers

The implications of market efficiency for investors are relatively well-defined. The implications for security analysts and investment advisers, although no less significant, are considerably more difficult to define. But whilst the effect on the former is essentially to delimit their investment strategy, for the latter, efficiency appears to threaten their very existence. One textbook on investment analysis notes: 'To many it may suggest that [the aspiring security analyst] is pursuing a career that has no real purpose or function.'[11] The authors continue, however:

> 'Yet all is not lost! It is the thousands of trained security analysts who are the eyes and ears of the efficient market. It is the industrious, probing, prying analyst who ensures that relevant information, and even rumour and hypothesis, is quickly reflected in the current price, and who by the collective might and chain reaction to prospective trends helps determine the future price. It is the inquisitive analyst . . . who by his (or her) actions or recommendations, helps bring a momentarily deviant price to its intrinsic value level.'[12]

But this is small comfort for the investment adviser specifically engaged and paid to assist his client investor to do better than average. Certainly, the statement emphasises the important fact that the market's pricing efficiency is not an adverse comment on the skill of individual investment advisers, but a favourable comment on the aggregate skill of the security analysts' profession. But the evidence nonetheless has uncomfortable implications for the analyst. If there are any experts who can systematically outperform the market sufficiently to compensate the investor for his incremental costs and risks, they are indeed very few.

A distinction may be drawn between the analyst who manages the funds of investors and the analyst who advises investors how to invest their funds. Given that the ultimate logic for investors is to buy the market, it would appear that the functions of both manager and adviser virtually disappear. But this is an oversimplification. Certainly, the role of the tipster, the analyst adviser who makes recommendations to his client to eschew the market portfolio and to adopt an inefficiently diversified position in pursuit of mispriced securities, cannot be defended in the face of the evidence. Even if there are a few gifted analysts whose skills have escaped the researcher, this is of little significance to the investor without some basis for distinguishing them from their less gifted colleagues. In addition, identification is insufficient if the very act of transmitting the advice becomes a piece of data that is likely to be rapidly reflected in the price, too rapidly for the advice to be operationally useful.

The implications for the two types of analysts will now be considered.

The Analyst as Adviser

Theory implies that the investor has no need for advice in the selection of securities. All investors in risky assets are directed to make broadly the same selection—the market portfolio—the only decision to be taken being the allocation of their capital between the portfolio and a riskless bond. And the latter decision is more an issue of subjective preference than a matter for external advice. However, in practice, resolution of the investment problem cannot always be so readily accomplished. In the first place, if the investor chooses to buy the market portfolio directly rather than through the medium of an index fund, then the portfolio will for practical reasons probably be a surrogate for the market, composed possibly of about 20 securities. The risk analysis required for both the construction and monitoring of such a portfolio will almost certainly call for expert advice.

In the second place, an investor's circumstances will frequently fail to fit precisely into the theoretically simple formula of buying and holding the market. It has been noted that those who fall into special tax categories, or who have specific maturity preferences, or have particular current income needs will require modification of the ideal formula, a process which for many will necessitate calling upon the services of an expert.

Finally, although there is a tendency frequently to associate financial advisers, and more particularly stockbrokers, with advice relating to the purchase and sale of securities, this is only one of many services undertaken by them. One writer observes that the range of services offered by the stockbroker is extremely wide,

'covering dealings in securities, the provision of analytical advice on companies and industries, the provision of research services to the corporate sector, the provision of corporate advice, dealing in gold, Krugerrand, and Kaffirs, dealers in foreign shares and currencies, providers of measurement of performance services and risk analysis services, advisers on modern portfolio theory, introducers of new companies to the market, fund managers for both private and institutional clients, tax advisers for private clients, tax advisers for institutions, dealers in gilts, Eurobonds, other foreign bonds, and other fixed interest investments, advisers to prospective mortgagees, property advisers, leasing specialists, advisers on hedging operations, ... promoters of venture capital schemes, economic advisers, insurance broking etc. etc.'[13]

Many of these services are clearly not significantly affected by the market's level of security pricing efficiency. Therefore, the financial adviser as distinct from the tipster can be assumed still to have a valid and important role to play.

The Analyst as Fund Manager

Market efficiency implies that the passive index fund will perform at least as well, and possibly better, than a managed fund, because the performance of the latter has to be sufficiently good to cover the costs of management.[14] This could be interpreted to mean that, like the tipster, the analyst manager has no place in the market. But if that is the case, if there are neither analysts to advise investors about mispriced securities, nor analysts to direct funds in pursuit of such securities, how then can the market remain efficient? In earlier chapters, a distinction was drawn between the general body of investors for whom efficiency implies a purely passive strategy and a minority of skilled professionals who can earn an economic return from trading in the minor inefficiencies of the market. But on the assumption that the skilled professional is unlikely personally to possess the amount of capital needed to finance such operations, then only if he is employed by the investment institutions will he be able effectively to perform his arbitrage role.

Is there any reason, however, why institutions should employ expert managers if the latter can do no more than cover their costs, any reason that is without invoking the argument that both institutions and managers need to be gulled into believing that the market is more inefficient than it actually is? To find an incentive, it is arguably sufficient simply to consider the alternative. If all major investment institutions ceased to use the services of any expert analysts and wholly pursued the passive strategy of holding the market portfolio, then presumably the market could decline into inefficiency, whereupon it would pay some institutions to re-employ the experts and draw funds away from those pursuing a purely passive strategy. Therefore, because the large institutions have a significant stake in the market, it would be self-defeating for them to abandon their monitoring role, particularly if there is no net cost to them. Because of their size, it is unlikely that the amount of funds needed for active trading would be a significant enough percentage of their total investment to have any material impact on their effective status as an index fund. It follows that it is not an active disbelief in the market's inefficiency that is a necessary condition for retaining the services of the expert trader but, rather, a recognition by some institutional investors, at least, that it is in their own interests actively to sustain the market's efficiency.

Some writers argue that even if the expert information processor does not advertise publicly the fruits of his research, but merely trades in his superior insights, the very act of being observed to buy securities may provide sufficient signal to the market to frustrate the analyst's ability to earn sufficient excess return to justify his activity.[15] There is, however, strong evidence that insiders can profit from their knowledge without their actions providing a totally revealing signal to the market,[16] although the two situations are not completely analogous, since the gifted adviser may be a more visible investor than the surreptitious insider. There is also some evidence that a few funds have been able consistently to cover their research costs.[17] More importantly, however, the issue raises unnecessary alarm about the marginal effects of efficiency. It cannot be a matter of concern both that the market may be too efficient to allow the expert to cover his costs, and at the same time that it may be incapable of remaining efficient unless the expert has the prospect at least of covering his costs. It is presumably one of the attributes of an efficient market that it can promote a mechanism for remunerating the agents upon which its efficiency depends.

In summary, although a positive role for experts appears to be incompatible with conditions of perfect efficiency, the professional analyst under near efficient conditions provides a vital contribution to market operations. His role is certainly no longer the consultant bargain-hunter as he tends to be portrayed in the conventional framework, but his contribution does not cease to be significant for that. If the truly competent expert presents a problem, it is, as will be shown in the concluding chapters, less one of identifying his role in the scheme of things than of making himself identifiable amongst a potentially large number of claimants to superior financial insight.

Conclusion

For an investor who believes that the securities market cannot be beaten except by chance, the optimal policy is to secure a position which minimises the chance of being beaten by the market, in effect to hold the market portfolio, where the latter consists of all marketable assets in the world in their value-related proportions. The fundamental lesson of efficient market theory, therefore, is that an investor's primary task is to maximise diversification and to minimise transaction costs.

Although the construction of the market portfolio may in practice have to be somewhat tailored to match the investor's taxation position, and although there are in addition certain practical problems in achieving and maintaining efficient international diversification, these problems can, for relatively low cost, be largely overcome by investing through an appropriate index fund. So, far from amounting to 'throwing in the towel', such a passive strategy, given the premise of efficiency, is the essence of good investment. The active element in investment strategy is contained in the process of determining the proportion of available funds to be allocated between the market portfolio and a risk-free government bond.

As for the role of investment advisers, an efficient market can be assumed to depend heavily upon the activities of skilled analysts and it can be argued that, even without the prospect of superior profits, there is a strong incentive for the major investment institutions to employ their services. In addition, ordinary investors will continue to need financial advice when their personal circumstances demand some individual tailoring of the theoretically optimal solution. Nonetheless, the conclusion is inescapable that the role of the analyst *qua* adviser is significantly modified, and in some respects significantly diminished by the market's efficiency. The notion that an investor can draw upon the analytical services of his broker, or his banker, or the financial press, or any other advisory agency, to secure a list of mispriced securities from which he can reasonably expect to profit, is irreconcilable both with the notion of efficiency and with the accumulated evidence. The role of the investment adviser is best perceived as fundamentally to assist less informed investors, not to beat the market, but to adapt its benefits to their personal circumstances. There is much to be done in that sphere, and it must ultimately serve advisers' own interests if they help to dispel the popular concept of the security analyst and the notion that a harvest of superior profits is there to be reaped.

Notes and References

1. For example, Belfer, N. (1965) states, 'overdiversification can result in mediocrity in investment results'; see 'Determining the construction of an individual securities portfolio', *Financial Analysts Journal*, May/June.
2. See, for example, Sharpe, W. (1963) 'A simplified model for portfolio analysis', *Management Science*, January.
3. Levy, H. and Sarnat, M. (1970) 'International diversification of investment portfolios', *American Economic Review*, September.
4. See Brealey, R. (1969) *An Introduction to Risk and Uncertainty from Common Stocks*, MIT Press.
5. In the UK, for instance, during the year 1982–3, the first £5,000 of capital gains were tax free.
6. 'Index Funds and Investment Strategy', (1976) American National Bank, Chicago.
7. *Weekly Staff Letter* (1975) December 18, D. Babson and Coy Inc, Boston, Mass.
8. Cohen J., Zinberg, E. and Ziekel, A. (1977) *Investment Analysis and Portfolio Management*, Irwin p. 755.
9. The Editor (1980) editorial—'Portfolio theory is inconsistent with the efficient market hypothesis', *Financial Analysts Journal*, September/October.
10. If the information relates to a change in risk class, the investor then would have to refer directly to the information to be able to adjust his portfolio and, therefore, his portfolio would remain out of balance until he personally receives the information. But it should be noted that it is his portfolio that is disrupted by the delay in receiving the information, not the share price mechanism.
11. Cohen, J., Zinberg, E. and Ziekel, A. *op. cit.* p. 29.
12. *Ibid.* p. 30.
13. Dennis, G. (1981) 'The current and future role of stockbrokers', *Investment Analyst*, October, p. 3.
14. For a managed portfolio to perform no worse than the market after costs, it has been estimated that the portfolio must outperform the market by 22% gross. See Ellis, C.D. (1975) 'The losers' game', *Financial Analysts Journal*, July/August, p. 15.
15. See Hirshleifer, J. and Riley, J. (1979) 'The analytics of uncertainty and information—an expository survey', *Journal of Economic Literature*, December, p. 1410.
16. For example, see Finnerty, J. (1976) 'Insiders and market efficiency', *Journal of Finance*, September.
17. e.g. see Mains, N.E. (1977) 'Risk, the pricing of capital assets, and the evaluation of investment portfolios: comment', *Journal of Business*, July.

8

The Implications for Corporate Financial Policy

Much of the early finance and management accounting literature had a tendency to perceive the firm's financing and investment decisions as exclusively the subjects of managers' preference and approval, and to treat the decision processes of shareholders in effect as a totally unrelated issue. It is, therefore, one of the major insights of modern finance theory to recognise the principle that the decisions of the firm cannot be taken without paramount regard for the decisions of its suppliers of capital.

The securities market is the interface between the company's managers and its investors, and the market's pricing efficiency is an important element in achieving effective communication between the two groups. But in addition to facilitating communication, an efficient market can affect the substance of the firm's decisions, and in certain areas may even eliminate the need for a decision.

The principal decision areas of the firm affected directly by market efficiency are (1) the timing of new issues, (2) the type of security issued, (3) the capital mix, (4) the maturity of securities, (5) capital budgeting, and (6) the cost of capital. Most of these issues are major topics in financial management theory and it is clearly not possible to address them fully. The purpose is to identify for each the more significant implications of market efficiency.

(1)   The Timing of New Issues

The traditional presumption of market inefficiency implies that new issues of capital should be carefully timed to coincide with the right conditions. Otherwise, if current prices are artificially low, the new subscribers will secure a share in the firm's existing assets on unduly favourable terms. The conventional advice, therefore, would be to delay the issue until the market gets the price right.

This kind of concern, however, makes little sense if the market is an efficient price-setter. Even if current prices are historically low, market efficiency implies that they are at their correct level, and that it is illusory to assume that they must be due for a recovery. Prices are low either because economic conditions are expected to have an adverse effect on future earnings, or because the cost of capital has risen. If the firm is presented, even under such inauspicious circumstances, with a new project which is expected to be sufficiently profitable to satisfy current cost of capital requirements, there is no virtue in delaying the project in the hope that financing conditions improve. The best estimate of a future share price is the current share price, and the best estimate of future costs of capital is captured in the yield of long-term securities, because, if efficiently priced, the latter will reflect the succession of short-term rates expected to prevail in the future.

A delay in making the issue might be defended on the grounds that the market's current perception of the company's future prospects may be incorrect if based on inadequate or misleading information. But this is a matter for more effective information disclosure. Any potential penalty befalling the company as a result of strong-form inefficiency is remedial by the company itself without having to wait for the market to ferret out the data.

Finally, it does not follow from what has been said that all projects worth undertaking should be undertaken immediately. Even if future economic conditions are fully reflected by current market prices, it may be more profitable to delay a project to coincide with certain foreseeable environmental conditions that happen to be more advantageous to the particular project. But this is quite a distinct matter from delaying the project to await better financing conditions. To pursue the latter course presupposes that the financial manager is better able than the market to predict the future course of stock prices and interest rates. If the market is efficient, this assumption is clearly unfounded.

(2) The Type of Security Issued

One of the byproducts of market inefficiency is the belief by some companies that it is possible to endow a security with certain ingredients that make it at the time cheaper to issue than alternatives. Convertible securities, for example, are designed allegedly to combine some of the advantages of debt and equity without incurring the corresponding disadvantages. The rationale of the convertible is that by introducing an equity element into a debt instrument it is possible to reduce the coupon rate to a more acceptable level. The coupon rate is, of course, simply the visible part of the cost, and if it were desirable *per se* to reduce the visible cost by inserting a hidden equity element, the logical policy would be to introduce a sufficient equity element to reduce the coupon to zero, namely to issue pure equity.

Two general observations may be made about any such attempt under efficient market conditions to bestow on a security features designed to lower the cost of capital:

(a) The security market trades in claims to future income streams, and market efficiency predicates a consistency in the pricing of the claims, irrespective of their form. The price per unit of risk is the same for all securities, and, therefore, there can be no intrinsically superior security.

(b) As long as the packaging of the two securities into a hybrid form can be replicated by investors by holding the individual components in their personal portfolios, the package should not sell at a price that is more than the weighted average of the respective components.

In effect, a security which is a combination of two classes of security is no more than that, and only if some investors wish to have, but for some reason, are unable to create their own combination, might there be a net advantage for the company to issue it. For example, certain trusts that are restricted to fixed income securities may perceive convertibles as a rear door into equity investment, and may be prepared to pay more than the sum of the individual parts. However, this does not signify pricing inefficiency, but simply the possible existence of a submarket for specialist classes of investors. Apart from that, however, a firm can only gain by dressing up a security into a particular package if it is able to fool new subscribers.

The possibility of fooling new subscribers is not a contradiction of the preceding discussion, because there is a clear division between the new issue market and the listed market itself. EMH relates to securities already being trading in the market. There is no evidence that the new issue market is efficient in the sense that issue prices necessarily reflect the intrinsic worth of the securities being issued. The issue price is set by a handful of advisers and the security purchased by a small fraction of the investment population. The setting of the price and the decision to subscribe are both susceptible to error. EMH implies only that when dealings in the security commence in the market, any error in the estimate of the semi-strong value will immediately be priced away.

(3)   The Capital Mix

Just as it is inconsistent with market efficiency for the firm to be able to reduce its cost of capital by packaging individual securities into a particular form, so it is if the firm packages its capital structure into a particular combination of debt and equity securities. One of the major contributions to finance theory was of course the demonstration by Modigliani and Miller[1] that the firm's cost of capital is insensitive to the capital mix. Market imperfections such as the taxation benefits to the company in issuing debt, and the taxation benefits to investors in buying equity,[2] together with transaction and bankruptcy costs, may make it possible for a particular capital structure to increase the value of the firm. But this is a different matter from being able to reduce the price of risk capital simply by mixing different classes of securities together. If market efficiency implies that no security is cheaper *per se* than any other, then the simple act of mixing securities cannot reduce their combined cost. This issue, however, will be more fully discussed in the subsequent section dealing with the measurement of the cost of capital.

(4)   The Maturity of Capital

Unlike equity securities, debt capital can be issued with varying degrees of maturity, ranging from one year to possibly thirty-year or more loans. Can a company benefit from choosing one maturity rather than another? It is clearly beneficial for a company to issue debt with a five-year life, say, if the funds are required for five years, since this avoids the transaction costs of issuing a series of shorter term bonds or the inconvenience and costs of calling in a bond of longer maturity. If the securities market is efficient, however, choosing the maturity for a bond that does not match the maturity of the investment on the grounds that the interest rate is lower, is misguided. If long-term rates, for instance, happen to be higher than short-term rates, this does not make them more expensive. The long-term rate should be higher if it correctly reflects an expectation of a future rise in short-term rates. Issuing a short-term bond to secure a lower coupon rate might appear to be beneficial in the short term, but when the time comes to replace it, short-term rates will, if expectations are fulfilled, have risen to a level such that the average cost over the period will be no less than that of the longer, apparently more expensive bond. Unnecessary transaction costs, however, will have been incurred in the process. In effect, market efficiency implies that the market is better able to predict the future course of interest rates than any individual financial manager. Maturities, therefore, should be chosen not to exploit observed differences in interest rates but to match the maturities of the investments which they are designed to finance.

(5)   Capital Budgeting

Despite the strong evidence favouring the security market's efficiency, it is surprising that there should be a general assumption amongst finance writers that the product market is fundamentally inefficient. This assumption is evidenced by the basic capital budgeting acceptance rule of modern investment theory, that projects should be selected only if they have a positive net present value.[3] For a project to have a positive NPV it must, by definition, have an expected return *in excess* of the acceptable rate for the risk class, otherwise it would have a zero NPV. In the securities market, by contrast, the significance of shares being 'correctly' priced is that they all have a zero NPV, offering no expectation of prospective excess returns. Whether the market for physical assets is so inefficient that all acceptable projects can be expected *ex ante* to generate excess profits is clearly a matter for debate, and seems unlikely to be true for competitive industries in developed countries. But the product market does not possess in the same measure the special characteristics of the securities market identified in Chapter 1 that mark the latter out as a likely candidate for pricing efficiency, particularly with respect to the level of competition and the degree of information disclosure. Given this, it is reasonable to assume that at least some productive investments provide bargain opportunities in the form of returns higher than the equilibrium minimum. The question at issue is what are the implications for capital budgeting decisions of the existence of an efficient securities market, given that the securities represent claims upon this inefficient and imperfectly competitive product market.

The implications are, of course, essentially derivations from the decision rules predicated for investors by market efficiency. Thus:

(a) The financial manager may ignore the individual risk-return preferences of the company's shareholders since they can create any desired risk-return position through their personal portfolios. Any project that earns an amount equal to or more than the return appropriate to its risk class is desirable whatever the personal risk preferences of the shareholders, because it is the market's price of risk that determines the project's contribution to the value of the firm.

(b) New investments can be selected without reference to the riskiness of the firm's existing investments. Until recently it was assumed that management needed to consider the total portfolio of the firm's investments in order to assess the relevant risk of any new investment.[4] This implied that a project could fall into one risk category if undertaken by company A and into another risk category if undertaken by company B, depending on the relative composition of the companies' other investments. It is now recognised, however, that the risk class of a project depends exclusively upon its relationship with the *market* portfolio, not the *firm's* portfolio. Hence its risk class is the same by whatever firm it is undertaken, and it can be validly assessed independently of any other investments that the particular firm is engaged upon.

(c) An extension of the latter principle is the important insight that it is not beneficial for a firm to engage in pure diversification on behalf of its shareholders. Investors, by holding the market portfolio, can diversify much more effectively than any company can. A company should of course undertake any project that creates new wealth for its shareholders even if this happens to lead it into a diversified position, but it is not the diversification effect that creates the wealth. In addition, there may be economies of scale in a conglomerate operation, or there may be behavioural benefits for management to diversify some of the firm's risk away, but it remains an important principle that risk diversification at the firm level produces no direct advantage for shareholders that cannot be achieved equally well in their personal portfolios.

(6) The Cost of Capital

Undoubtedly, it is in respect of its impact on the cost of capital issue that market efficiency has had its greatest significance, since it is via the cost of capital mechanism that the effects of efficiency are transmitted into the internal decision-making procedures of the firm. The term 'cost of capital' is used frequently to signify both the firm's overall cost of capital and the cut-off rate for specific investments, but the need for a more precise definition will emerge in the subsequent discussion.

The riskiness of a firm's prospective investments can be reflected in the evaluation procedure in one of two ways, either by means of a coefficient applied directly to the projected cash flows to reduce them to their certainty-equivalents,[5] or through an upward adjustment of the discount rate and so effect the conversion into certainty-equivalence through the discounting process.[6] But, whichever of the two methods is used, the essential problem is the same—how to elicit from the market place the ruling price of risk as it affects individual investments. For convenience, the discussion will focus on the risk-adjusted discount rate technique.

There are two possible approaches to discovering the appropriate cut-off rate for a specific investment:

(a) formulate a general model for the price of risk and apply it to the investment under review; or

(b) seek out a twin investment for which the cut-off rate is known or more readily ascertainable.

If the market is inefficient, only the second approach is feasible, because, in the absence of a consistent price for risk, no general formula can be derived. But even under the second approach, an inefficient market implies that there is no assurance that the listed security of any company, other than the one undertaking the investment, will be priced on the same return-to-risk ratio as is appropriate for the investment, even though such a security might be in every respect the perfect twin. Hence, the traditional assumption has been that the best match is the package of securities issued, or to be issued, by the company itself. Therefore, the firm's weighted average cost of capital has been conventionally advanced as the appropriate yardstick. This approach has received further support from the assumption that the firm might be able to influence the cut-off rate for its investments by arranging its capital structure in a particular fashion. Minimisation of the cost of capital is still advanced by many writers,[7] as a valid goal of the firm, giving rise to the perceived need to compute the firm's overall cost of capital.

The Weighted Average Cost of Capital concept, therefore, is very much rooted in an assumption of market inefficiency and one of the great advantages of having an efficient market, as will be demonstrated shortly, is that it effectively dispenses with the need for WACC, since it suffers from certain fundamental defects that in practice render it virtually inoperative. The underlying concept of finding a twin security to match the firm's investment is sound, but paradoxically the firm's own parcel of securities will rarely, if ever, mirror any of its individual investments.

Thus, the cost of capital k for any asset is composed of two elements:

$$k = i + b$$

where
    i = the risk-free rate (the pure price of time)
    b = the premium for risk

But i (and possibly b) varies with the maturity of the asset. The yield of a one-year bond may be significantly different from that of an otherwise comparable five-year bond, not because it is any cheaper or more expensive, but because future short-term rates are expected to vary, and the longer term yield reflects the average of these future short-term rates. Therefore, the return k on any risky asset depends on its maturity no less than its risk.

This implies that for the overall weighted average cost of capital of a firm to be relevant to any specific investment[8] the following conditions must hold:

(1) The investment must have the same risk as the average risk of the firm; and
(2) The maturity of the investment must be the same as the maturity of the firm's capital structure.

It is conceivable that, for a few firms, all current and prospective investments will fall into the same risk class, but it is virtually inconceivable that the second condition should hold. Equity is a perpetuity and most debt capital has a finite maturity. Hence the average rate derived from the mix of such maturities cannot be relevant to any specific investment, whatever its maturity. In effect, if the term structure of interest rates is a material factor in the determination of yields, the only firm whose cost of capital could validly be used for assessing its investments would be a pure equity company engaged in perpetual investments with common risk. But, by definition, the weighted average cost of capital implies that more than one security has been issued by the company, and must, therefore, always be irrelevant, unless by chance the term structure curve happens to be horizontal and the rate of interest for all maturities equal.

Given its inherent defects, then, why is the firm's cost of capital still used by textbook writers, particularly when so many appear to accept the market's pricing efficiency as given? Partly it seems because, despite the pioneering work of Modigliani and Miller[9] in demonstrating that the investment cut-off rate depends solely on the risk characteristics of the investment and not on the method of financing, the notion that a firm can interpose its financial policies between the securities market and its own investments, in such a way as to modify the impact on the market's price of time and risk, has tended to retain a hold on orthodox finance teaching. And the durability of this notion can be attributed principally to a failure to define the cost of capital precisely and, in particular, to distinguish clearly between the interest cost of capital and the transaction costs of capital.

Defining the Cost of Capital

The cost of capital as a term of art in capital budgeting has come to denote a composite of two distinct categories of cost: (i) transaction costs, such as flotation costs, bankruptcy costs and the taxation effects of debt, all of these being the effects of market imperfections; and (ii) the interest cost, being the pure price of time i and risk b. Although the two categories are quite distinguishable and separable, there has been a tradition to treat them jointly, dating from the original analysis of Modigliani and Miller,[10] through to many contemporary writers.[11] The cost of equity k_e, for example, is frequently adjusted upwards to reflect flotation costs[12] and the cost of debt k_i downwards by the factor $(1 - t)$ to reflect the tax privileges of debt, implying that the firm's debt holders have a required rate of return of only $k_i(1 - t)$.

The arithmetic justification for this device of adjusting the cost of debt by the factor $(1 - t)$ depends on the expected cash flows of the investment being measured as if there were no tax relief for debt. But it is quite feasible to adopt a different technique, namely to incorporate all transaction costs directly into the cash flows, and to leave the discount rate as a pure measure of the interest cost. Some writers argue that the alleged superiority of this second approach is only a matter of semantics.[13] But arguably it is more than that. The fundamental objection to the first method is not the pedagogic one that it incorrectly suggests to the casual observer that, since the composite cost of capital number is reducible by the firm's financial policies, it may be possible to reduce the interest cost of capital. The real objection is that the method ties the company inescapably into the use of the firm's weighted average cost of capital. By contrast, the alternative approach of adjusting the project's cash flows for all transaction costs of capital, isolates the interest cost problem and opens up a direct link between the investment and the market. Given an efficient market, it is possible, in principle at least, for either the formula or the matching technique to be applied directly to the investment, the one through the Capital Asset Pricing Model, the other by pairing the investment with a twin security listed in the market which matches the investment in risk and maturity. Neither approach is, of course, without considerable practical difficulties. But then neither is the firm's weighted average cost of capital, except that it suffers from the more fundamental objection already discussed that, even if the practical difficulties could be overcome, the figure that emerges would almost certainly be irrelevant.

A Firm Cannot Minimise its Interest Cost of Capital

The essential lesson of market efficiency, therefore, is that the interest cost of capital is purely market determined and cannot be modified by the firm through its financial policies. It is the same discount rate for a given investment whatever company undertakes it. To understand why a well-established company should pay the same cost of capital as a relative newcomer, it is useful to distinguish between the concept of a *project* and that of an *investment*. A project is a business idea, the construction of a hotel, or the establishment of a steel plant. An investment, on the other hand, is a configuration of cash flows. It is investments that are discounted not projects. Figure 8.1 illustrates how two firms presented with the same project X may generate quite distinct cash flow configurations, A_p and A_q, as a result of one having greater operating efficiency, or lower flotation costs, or a better taxation shield by virtue of its debt capital. But once the cash flows are established, then, and only then, is an investment created. The well established firm may not only have produced higher cash flows, it may even have lowered their variability in the process. If

Determining factors

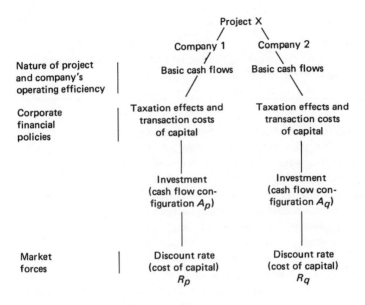

Figure 8.1   *Firms can affect the investment class of a project, but not the cost of capital for an investment*

so, the investment A_p may attract a lower discount rate R_p than that of A_q. But this is not to say that company 1 has reduced the cost of capital *vis-à-vis* company 2. Company 1 has created out of project X an investment with a lower risk rating than that of company 2. But it is not in the power of either company to affect the discount rate appropriate to that or any other investment's risk class.

Measuring the Cost of Capital

Both the problems of identifying the risk class of an investment and of determining the amount of the risk premium are precisely the issues addressed by the Capital Asset Pricing Model, which is not only the logical derivative of market efficiency, but the most complete framework for measuring the impact of risk yet conceived. The investment class of the project is represented by its 'beta', which is a statistical measure of the sensitivity of the investment's returns to those of the market portfolio.

The return required for an individual investment j is given by the expression:

$$R_j = R_f + \beta_j (R_m - R_f)$$

where

R_m = the return on the market portfolio of all risky assets

R_f = the riskless rate of interest

β_j = a measure of how the returns on the investment vary with the returns on the market

There are, it should be stressed, very real problems in applying this model for risk to individual investments. The measurement of an investment's beta is far from straightforward, because it depends on being able to measure the sensitivity of the project's returns to those of the market portfolio.[14] But the market portfolio cannot be identified precisely[15] and, for the same reason, R_m is not an observable statistic. In addition, CAPM is a single-period model and this limits its applicability to multi-period investments.

But even if these difficulties were interpreted as sufficient to reject CAPM as an operational tool for measuring the market's price of risk, this does not affect the conclusion that the firm's weighted average cost of capital is fundamentally defective. In addition to the theoretical objections already made, the measurement of WACC is itself dependent on CAPM, or some appropriate model for risk, in calculating the costs of the individual components.[16]

If no such acceptable model exists, financial managers have no choice but to fall back on the second of the two approaches—the matching technique—and to seek out a security which at least matches the investment's maturity. In the final analysis, until a more operational model is available, a subjectively derived premium for risk can be added to the objectively verifiable riskless rate.

The Cost of Capital and the Quantity of Finance Raised

The final issue concerns the implications of market efficiency for the intuitively appealing view that a rapidly expanding company cannot raise unlimited amounts of capital without having to pay an increasingly higher cost for its funds. Thus, some writers postulate an upward sloping supply curve for capital for individual firms, as in Figure 8.2, implying that the firm's cost of capital rises with the amount of capital raised.[17] The argument is that if a firm attempts to raise an unusually large amount of

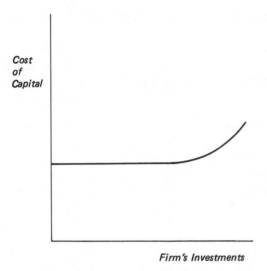

Figure 8.2   *Supply curve of capital*

finance in relation to its size, the market will raise the cost until the firm successfully demonstrates its ability to digest the capital.

This, of course, implies that the cost of capital for an individual investment may vary depending on whether the company happens to be expanding too quickly or not, and, therefore, is in direct conflict with the principle that the cost of capital for an investment is independent of the specific company. How is it possible to reconcile the market's efficiency in pricing risk with the apparently reasonable assumption that a firm is unlikely to be able to raise limitless amounts of capital without incurring some form of penalty, setting aside the possibility that a particular firm may be so large that its demand for capital could affect the market's aggregate demand position.

Two explanations are possible:

(a) The rapid expansion may have the effect of inducing greater variability in the cash flows of the firm's projects. It has already been noted that the impact of a firm's policies or circumstances on a particular project may be such as to transform the project into an investment class with a higher level of risk than it might have had if undertaken by another firm, leading as a result to a higher cost of capital. This, however, is quite a different matter from suggesting that the market charges a higher rate of interest for a specific investment or set of investments simply because they are being undertaken by an expanding firm. It is the investment class that has changed, not the price of risk.

(b) Even if the rapid expansion in reality does not affect the variability of the firm's cash flows, it may be perceived by the market to do so. The act of raising large amounts of capital may signal to the market the possibility that the management will not be able to handle the growth smoothly. If this fear is in fact misplaced, it could be concluded that the market is inefficient in the strong sense but not necessarily in the semi-strong sense. If the market's fears are reasonable in relation to the information given to it, its response could be perfectly consistent with semi-strong efficiency. The fact that it charges an excessive interest rate when viewed in the context of the total information set reflects the inadequacy of the firm's information disclosure practices rather than the market's pricing efficiency. The lesson is that, in an efficient market, it is in the interests of the firm to publish adequate information about its investment plans, so that the return required by its suppliers of capital is based on the true risk of its investments and not on some misguided estimate derived from imperfect signals.

It has been noted that the company may suffer if its information flow to the market is inadequate or misleading. Arguably, of course, there may be an opportunity for gain if the lack of information happens to cause the market's perception of the company's condition to be unduly favourable. Should it, for example, make a new issue to take advantage of the fact that the market currently overestimates the attractiveness of its shares *vis-à-vis* other securities, rather than issue the appropriate information to correct the market's misperception? In effect, is the market's semi-strong efficiency a condition to be enjoyed by the firm and its strong-form inefficiency a condition to be exploited?

Whatever management in practice might perceive to be the appropriate answer to that question, one important principle should be recognised. The effect of semi-strong efficiency is to make holding the market portfolio, and not just that individual company's securities, the appropriate strategy for most investors. Their welfare, therefore, in the end is dependent on the success of the market portfolio, and transcends the ability of individual companies actively to promote and exploit inefficiencies in the market.

Apart from it being unlikely that a company will be able to secure any short-term gain from its deceptions without paying a price for it in the long term in the form of lower credibility, the market portfolio perspective significantly diminishes the validity of the traditional emphasis on pursuing the interests of *existing shareholders* versus all others. Holders of the market portfolio may also hold the firm's debt instruments, and new security-holders become existing security-holders. The goal is not to promote the interests of one section and one generation of security-holders above all others. It is more consistent with the philosophy of market portfolio theory that firms both respond to and actively seek to promote market efficiency in its fullest sense.

Conclusion

The securities market is the medium of communication between the suppliers of capital and their agents. Just as market efficiency implies that the suppliers should accept rather than seek to exploit the market's prices, so it implies that the agents should accept rather than seek to exploit its signals. The fundamental lesson for financial managers, therefore, is that the creation of corporate wealth is substantially independent of the firm's interaction with the securities market, but depends almost exclusively on the identification and execution of profitable productive investments. There is no intrinsically superior type of security or combination of securities which can be used to finance investments. There is no time for issuing securities which is more opportune than any other. Finally, the price of time and risk and, therefore, the benchmark for evaluating investment projects, is determined solely in the market place, and not only applies equally to all companies in the market, but is incapable of being affected by them.

Notes and References

1. Modigliani, F. and Miller, M.H. (1958) 'The cost of capital, corporation finance and the theory of investment', *American Economic Review*, June.
2. See Miller, M. (1977) 'Debt and taxes', *Journal of Finance*, May.
3. See Van Horne, J. (1980) *Financial Management and Policy*, Prentice-Hall, p. 115.

4. For example, see earlier editions such as the third edition of Van Horne, *ibid.* (1974) p. 173.
5. Robichek, A. and Myers, S.C. (1966) 'Conceptual problems in the use of risk-adjusted discount rates', *Journal of Finance*, December.
6. See Weston, J.F. and Brigham, E. (1981) *Managerial Finance*, Holt-Saunders, p. 475.
7. See, for example, Brealey, R. and Myers, S. (1981) *Principles of Corporate Finance*, McGraw-Hill, p. 362.
8. See Keane, S. (1978) 'The cost of capital as a financial decision tool', *Journal of Business Finance and Accounting*, Autumn.
9. *op. cit.*
10. Modigliani, F. and Miller, M.H. (1963) 'Corporate income taxes and the cost of capital: a correction', *American Economic Review*, June.
11. See Weston and Brigham, *op. cit.* Ch. 16.
12. *Ibid.* p. 702.
13. See Partington, G.H. (1979) 'The tax-deductibility of interest payments and the weighted average cost of capital: a comment', *Journal of Business Finance*, Spring.
14. See Van Horne, J., *op. cit.* Ch. 8.
15. Roll, R. (1977) 'A critique of the asset pricing theory's tests: Part I', *Journal of Financial Economics*, March.
16. See Copeland, T.E. and Weston, J.F. (1979) *Financial Theory and Corporate Policy*, Addison Wesley, Ch. 11.
17. See Weston and Brigham, *op. cit.* pp. 620–3.

9

The Implications for Financial Reporting

One conclusion emerges beyond reasonable doubt from the empirical evidence relating to market efficiency: it is futile for the ordinary layman without access to privileged information to expect to gain anything from looking behind the market price of securities. Whatever doubts one might have about the opportunities open to the expert investor, the market's pricing efficiency has unambiguously been established by research as sufficient to preclude the layman, on the basis of his own insights, from systematically profiting from the search for mispriced securities. It follows that some consideration needs to be given to the relevance of the conventional objective ascribed to financial reports as that of informing the investment decisions of the ordinary shareholder.

It is stressed at the outset that the interests of only one user group, investors, will be considered here, since they are the principal beneficiaries of market efficiency. The conclusions that will be drawn for financial reporting practice may, therefore, conflict with the interests of other user groups, but the significance of conflict amongst financial reporting users is a matter for separate discussion. The object of this chapter is simply to identify the principal implications of market efficiency for those affected directly by it.

Focusing exclusively on the investor group is, however, more than a question of convenience. Although it has become common practice for financial reporting theorists to emphasise the multiplicity of potential users,[1] it is essential for theory development, particularly when confronted with such a significant matter as market efficiency, that the financial reporting needs of each major group be considered initially in isolation before any attempt is made to construct an integrated solution. There is little justification in assuming *a priori* that a single general purpose report is the ideal solution, without allowing for the possibility that one or more groups may require a solution substantially and irreconcilably different from the rest.

Investors' Information Needs

Investors' needs can be assumed to depend materially on the environment in which they operate. Securities can be traded (a) in an unlisted market, (b) in a listed market perceived to be inefficient and (c) in a listed market perceived to be efficient.

Unlisted Market

For securities not listed on any organised market, the investor may be assumed to require information for three purposes:

  (i)   to monitor management's stewardship
  (ii) to determine the value of the securities, and
  (iii) to estabish a price for exchange purposes.

The corporate financial report is likely to form the principal source of information to the shareholder for each of the above purposes.

Inefficient Listed Market

In a listed market generally believed to be inefficient in setting prices, the investor's decision needs are confined to the first two purposes, monitoring stewardship, and assessing value. The market is the price-setter, and although the investor's decision to buy-hold-or-sell may be influenced by the market's price, he cannot normally influence the latter. This is the environment postulated by those who subscribe to conventional theory. Investors' primary task in these conditions is to arrive at a valuation which can be compared to the market price and lead accordingly to a buy-hold-sell decision.

Efficient Market

If the market is an efficient price-setter, then price and value become synonymous. The ordinary investor can accept the prices as given and can substantially limit his investigations to stewardship assessment. The market becomes both price-setter and valuer.

Financial Reporting Philosophy

Whilst the primary objective of the corporate report is essentially to influence the investment decisions of existing and prospective security-holders, the information content of the report may be partly or wholly characterised by one of two accounting philosophies, depending on which of the above environments holds: (a) decision-output accounting, where the overriding objective is to provide the user with an accounting simulation of his perceived decision needs, and (b) decision-input accounting, where the fundamental objective is to provide the user with the data inputs needed for making his decisions.

Decision-Output Accounting

Under this regime, the accountant acts in a quasi-judicial capacity insofar as his basic role is interpreted as providing a structured answer to the users' decision problems. The accountant's intermediation between the raw data and the user is very positive. He discards information which he considers inappropriate, chooses between alternative accounting measurement systems, and finally refines and processes the residual data into an integrated overview of the firm's financial position.

The quasi-judicial approach is enshrined in the UK statutory requirement that accounts should show a 'true and fair view', implying that reports should contain not just the basic data for the user to process but a *view*, in particular management's view, of the company's profit and financial state of affairs. The financial report is seen as essentially solution-oriented in character, consisting primarily of an accounting model that mirrors the user's decision model. Hence the corner-stone of the report is to be found in the income and position statements, with appendices, footnotes and supplementary statements being looked upon as no more than explanatory adjuncts of those primary statements. Success is measured more in terms of the extent to which these primary statements answer satisfactorily the questions which users are assumed to be seeking to resolve, than with whether the information disclosed provides adequate evidence for users who wish to answer the questions for themselves. At the extreme, it is essentially 'bottom-line' accounting.

The principal issues of mainstream accounting theory spring from a decision-output accounting framework: income measurement, depreciation, treatment of goodwill, inflation accounting, etc., that is those issues which are concerned primarily with the problems of making the reported view an apt and credible *assessment* of the firm's activities. The user is viewed essentially as a consumer rather than a processor of information.

Decision-Input Accounting

The alternative philosophy is where accounting is viewed primarily as evidential in purpose. The role of the accountant is fundamentally that of an expert witness, and the financial report a data source to serve as the input to the user's decision. The accountant's role is, therefore, much more passive than that of its judicial counterpart. Although he will be obliged to form a view in respect of specific items such as estimates for realisable values, replacement costs, etc. and in respect of general matters such as the standard of disclosure, a pure evidential approach would no more expect the accountant to articulate an overall view or assessment of the firm's position than a court of law would expect an expert witness to express his view about the outcome of the case. It is not his function to attempt to anticipate the user's decision. The critical aspect of financial reporting is the adequacy and relevance of information disclosure, not the manner of presentation or method of integration.

The main theoretical issues are concerned with matters such as identification of users' decision needs, cash flow accounting, forecast data, segmental reporting, etc. The conventional income and position statements are, at best, potential additions to the evidential base[2] and, at worst, a veil over the raw material of the data source. Although some recognisable format would undoubtedly be desirable, it might matter little whether the relevant information is disclosed in footnotes or incorporated into the principal statements. It matters considerably, however, that relevant evidence might be omitted altogether, if the specific accounting measures happen not to be in harmony with the accounting measurement system selected for the principal statements.

Financial reports, of course, in reality are rarely wholly judicial or evidential in character. The two philosophies are almost universally intertwined in both the practice and theory of financial reporting. They do, however, represent two potentially extreme and conflicting views about the nature and purpose of financial reports which could have a significant impact on reporting policy.

The history of financial reporting can be interpreted as consisting of a gradual evolution from a largely decision-output approach towards a more evidential orientation. Early financial statements had a marked bottom-line emphasis, designed to establish the profit for the year and the net worth of the equity, but frequently revealing very little else that could enlighten the user as to the composition of these succinct judgments. Over time, however, the intervention of regulatory agencies has been directed as much towards increased disclosure of the relevant financial numbers for the decision-maker to use, as towards finding a consistently acceptable accounting method, indicating a growing respect for the decision-input aspect of financial reporting.

The evolutionary process can be attributed, to some extent at least, to the emergence of a sophisticated securities market, given the assumption that the choice between the two approaches depends largely on the capacity of the user to handle the data. When a financial reporting philosophy first developed, there was no organised securities market to speak of, and ordinary shareholders depended heavily on the expertise of the reporting accountant to help fulfil the role of a market in pricing and valuing their securities. At the extreme, the ideal financial report for the unskilled layman would have been the pure judicial statement: share value = n.

The User's Level of Expertise

The establishment of an organised securities market, albeit commonly perceived to be inefficient as a price-setter, and the subsequent increase in the level and diversity of accounting sophistication, necessitated a judgment about the level of expertise appropriate for financial reports. The option ranged from the naive layman to the highly professional analyst, but, in the interests of equity, convention settled on the 'informed and diligent layman',[3] a formula which retained the necessity of pursuing a fundamentally decision-output framework, but which allowed the addition of more detailed and complex supportive data.

The potential conflict created by the informed layman user hypothesis in respect of the two accounting philosophies is exemplified in recent efforts to come to terms with accounting for inflation. Those who favour a more decision-output orientation for financial reports have tended to place considerable emphasis on the identification of a single, internally consistent method of capturing the effects of inflation so that the end products of profit and net worth can be satisfactorily measured and represented. Those who subscribe more to the evidential approach attach more significance to the disclosure of the relevant price-level numbers than to the form or consistency of presentation.

It is obvious that this gradual movement towards a decision-input philosophy is likely to be accelerated if market efficiency becomes more widely accepted. The implications of semi-strong efficiency are that the ordinary shareholder has no need to study financial reports to determine the worth of his shares. The market is the price-setter, and its efficiency implies that it is a highly skilled information processor. Hence the conventional reporting target of the layman seeking a value for his investment ceases to be appropriate. The relevant audience becomes the market, assumed for practical purposes to be composed of experts.

Of course, since we do not know precisely the mechanism by which security prices are determined, it is arguable that the diligent layman contributes to the price-setting process, in which case addressing financial data primarily to the professional community could conceivably disrupt the market's efficiency. Two points, however, should be noted:

(1) If the market were known to be efficient, there would be little attraction for the layman to pursue his diligent analysis of published data in search of mispriced securities. Possibly only a small number of experts would earn sufficient 'rent' from their dealings in the market to compensate for their efforts.

(2) If the market became inefficient as a result of the layman's withdrawal from active participation, the inefficiencies would be known to exist only if the remaining professional community recognised their existence. It would be reasonable to expect that the subsequent exploitation of the inefficiencies would reduce them to a scale that was again sufficient only to compensate the experts for their labours.

Market Efficiency and the Content of Financial Reports

If the market's efficiency can help identify the relevant user of financial reports, the question arises to what extent does it help determine which specific accounting numbers users wish to be included in the reports. Directly, it provides very little insight into the specific information required, but indirectly, the assumption of efficiency enables researchers to use the Capital Asset Pricing Model to test the relationship between certain specific accounting numbers and security prices. For various reasons, however, some of which we have already encountered in earlier chapters, this approach has only a limited scope for deciding what information is most useful.[4]

An illustration of the limitations of the approach is provided by recent studies of the impact on prices of the requirement to publish current cost statements in corporate financial reports.[5] The findings have tended to indicate the absence of any perceptible market response, and this has given rise to some controversy about the appropriate interpretation. A number of explanations are possible:

(1) *The market has failed to respond to relevant information and is therefore inefficient.*

This is a possible but somewhat simplistic interpretation, partly because it does not accord with other findings of market responsiveness, and partly because, as shown below, a non-response to the *publication* of current cost data may, if anything, be supportive of rather than inimical to market efficiency.

(2) *Current costs are not relevant to the market's needs.*

This interpretation may be consistent with the findings, but it is certainly far from conclusive. If current cost data are relevant to the valuation of shares, then even a part-efficient market will strive to make adjustments to historic cost accounts, if these are all it is given, in an effort to derive current cost perspectives. The more efficient the market is, the more accurate will its estimates be, and, as a result, the changeover to current cost accounting will be less likely to produce an observable impact on share prices. Therefore, the absence of positive results to the tests can equally be interpreted as implying that the market is highly efficient in guessing the effects of inflation etc. This would not imply that current cost information is irrelevant, but it does raise the possibility as to whether current cost accounting in financial reports is worthwhile, given that the market appears to be able independently to derive effective assessments of current costs from historic cost data. In effect, current cost data may be relevant, but its publication by firms may be superfluous. Once again, however, this interpretation, while consistent with the evidence, is far from compelling. There is yet another possible interpretation.

(3) *The market's estimates of the effects of current costs based on historic costs are on average good estimates, but its estimates for individual firms may contain errors owing to an insufficient information base in the financial reports.*

If these individual errors are random they will be diversified away in aggregate market prices, and this will account for the failure of the tests to reveal any apparent market response to current cost data. If this final interpretation is valid, the implication is that the publication of current cost accounts, while not affecting aggregate prices, may affect the prices of individual companies *vis-à-vis* one another. Publication of current cost accounts may therefore be important for individual companies in bridging the gap between their semi-strong and strong worth.

Yet the market is unable to provide the necessary signals to confirm this interpretation. Why is this? The reason lies in the problems of researching the market outlined in Chapter 2. It is a near impossible task to relate the price movements of individual securities with specific events or information data. There are potentially too many events affecting the value of a company at any given point in time to be confident that an observed price movement is in response to a specific item of information. A large sample is needed to diversify away observational errors. But a large sample implies that any correctional adjustments which the market makes at the time the financial reports are presented will tend to cancel one another out unless the errors in the market's estimates are non-random. For these reasons the effects of the publication of current cost data may be imperceptible to the market researcher. But imperceptibility in these circumstances does not signify insignificance.

It is probably safe to conclude, therefore, that although an efficient market may offer some insights into which accounting numbers should be included in a financial report, it has a very restricted contribution to make in this respect. It is unlikely that the relevant numbers will ever be fully determined without drawing extensively on intuitive, theoretical and analytical sources.

These limitations, however, are not to say that market efficiency is without significant implications for the content of financial reports. If it offers inadequate guidelines in determining the specific accounting items that should be included, its implication for the appropriate quality of the information are far-reaching. Arguably, whether a decision-input or decision-output orientation is relevant, the appropriate subject-matter for financial reporting to investors is primarily the same. It is the level of comprehension and the degree of information-processing that differentiates the financial report under efficient market conditions from its traditional counterpart.

The implications of the expert-user assumption inherent in market efficiency is that no relevant information should ever be withheld simply because it might not be fully understood by some users. This, of course, conflicts with traditional reporting philosophy. It is quite conceivable, indeed, that the significance of some relevant information might not even be understood fully by the individual accountants responsible for its publication, but which could nonetheless be of value to the professional investment community. This should not inhibit publication. Nor should financial reports necessarily be limited to a single accounting measurement system. The traditional emphasis on producing an acceptable and credible measure of profit and financial position has placed a premium on the use of one internally consistent accounting method. As a result, theoreticians have focused their researches on finding the best method available to satisfy their concept of profit and financial position. The fact, however, that several competing methods have variously been presented as candidates for this role suggests the possibility that there may be informational content in more than one, and perhaps several accounting systems. If efficiency implies that the market has substantially outgrown its dependency on decision-output accounting, it may be of little significance whether the market receives several balance sheets, or indeed any balance sheet, provided the relevant information is issued in some form to enable it to perform its information-processing function. It may require part, but only part of several accounting systems, each with its own perspective, to give the market the insight it needs to perform that function effectively.

The solution of reporting on a multi-accounting basis may be interpreted by some as an abdication of accounting choice. This interpretation is, of course, valid only from a decision-output perspective. Within the decision-input framework of efficient markets, it reflects a simple recognition that the exclusive use of one particular accounting method may fail to serve the market's requirements. If the result is the absence of any end-product within the report other than an apparently disparate collection of financial data, this is a recognition of the fact that the relevant decision is not within the financial report itself but in the market place, namely in the share price.

Finally, market efficiency implies that the content of financial reports should reflect an earlier stage of the information-production process. The essential characteristic of any decision process is the transformation of raw data into some form of final adjudication. The more active the information user is in the decision-making process, the nearer to the raw material it is desirable for him to be. Financial reports could conceivably, therefore, range in their content from ostensibly unstructured schedules of raw accounting numbers to highly processed, articulated accounting statements, depending on the degree of decision-making participation to which the reader is assumed to be committed. The logic of market efficiency is that the role of the accountant changes from its traditional processing function of preparing for the layman a relatively concise and unambiguous view of the profit and position of the firm, to that of identifying and transmitting to the market the data input for the latter to process. Disclosure rather than accounting method, substance rather than form, become the critical issues.

Specific Reporting

In the introduction to this chapter, the possibility was envisaged that radically different financial reporting solutions might be desirable for different user groups. The conclusion, however, goes even further, in that it may be found necessary for the major user group of conventional theory to be itself divided for financial reporting purposes. Investors in the listed market have a twofold informational need: as overseers of management and as price-takers. But in the second context at least, their need for information is not personal, but indirect. It matters little to the ordinary shareholder whether he himself reads or can comprehend the information. His interests lie in the free flow of relevant information to the market, possessing as far as possible the qualities described above, so that the share price closely approximates its intrinsic value (strong worth). The expert in the process gains no advantage over the layman. He makes the market efficient for the latter, earning a reward sufficient only to compensate him for his efforts.

Stewardship Report

An efficient market is not in itself sufficient to justify preparing a separate stewardship report for the ordinary shareholder. It demands only that a market report be issued unconstrained by any of the ordinary investor's limitations in understanding. Whether a special and more structured set of statements should be prepared for ordinary investors remains a matter of dispute, depending on the view one takes about the rights and responsibilities the ordinary shareholder has to oversee personally the stewardship of management. To the extent that stewardship assessment can never be complete without some formulation of future prospects, then arguably any attempt to divide the reporting function may be misleading and counter-productive, in which case the interests of the ordinary shareholder would possibly best be served by addressing all relevant financial information to the expert.

Against that, it is arguably inherent in the voting power of equity stock that the holder have a reasonable opportunity to exercise his judgment and to formulate a view on management's performance. It may be both unrealistic and dangerous to limit communications to a level comprehensible only to the financial expert. In this case, a separate stewardship report addressed to the diligent and well-informed layman would be desirable.

Portfolio Information

Investors' potential interest in information was earlier described as threefold. It is possible, however, to identify a fourth category of information, that relating to the construction of an efficient portfolio. Although portfolio evaluation remains a matter that must be taken account of in the investment decision even in an efficient market, it would be unrealistic to suggest that the assessment of a particular company's portfolio characteristics could be undertaken by the layman. Portfolio-related data are too technical to be usefully directed other than to an expert. Although this compels the layman to seek expert guidance in the construction of his portfolio, no serious disadvantage can be claimed since, it will be recalled, the portfolio construction can readily be achieved through the agency of expertly managed index funds.

The Unlisted Company

Only a small proportion of all companies are listed in the market, and hence market efficiency may have little relevance to the reporting practices of the majority. Shareholders in an unlisted company have no ready price or value to which they can refer, and the accounts issued by the company are likely to be for them the prime source of information. If the informed layman remains the appropriate level of expertise, then the traditional style of accounts may continue to be relevant. Clearly, the accounting practices of listed companies will exert a certain influence over those of unlisted companies, but it is important that the two groups be treated quite separately by regulatory disclosure agencies, if an adequate response to the market's needs is to be achieved.

Insider Dealing

It has been argued that one of the particular benefits of achieving a state where security prices reflect their strong worth is that it thwarts the activities of the unscrupulous insider. Hence the desirability of full disclosure. Some writers, however, argue that if the labour market were efficient, the remuneration of insiders would be adjusted downwards to reflect their opportunities to exploit their privileged position. They would, therefore, receive no significant net advantage from their position, but would nevertheless contribute to the market's efficiency by driving security prices towards their strong worth.

From a purely economic viewpoint it is possible to ascribe this positive role to insider dealing, but in practice it seems unlikely that the rewards from insider transactions could ever be measured or controlled in such a way that equity was achieved, and seen to be achieved. In addition, as long as insider trading is regarded socially as potentially unjust, it is no less likely that corporate officers in responsible positions will be paid a premium to discourage them from engaging in insider transactions. There is certainly evidence of some delay between the occurrence of inside events and the adjustment of the share price. To depend on the self-interested pursuits of informed insiders is unlikely ever to be as acceptable or effective a mechanism for achieving strong efficiency as direct and prompt disclosure to the market.

Disclosure Regulation

Recognition of the need for greater disclosure to the market does not necessarily imply the need for greater regulatory intervention. Whether the increased disclosure should be attained by the free operation of the market or by regulation is not the issue here. The crucial lesson of market efficiency is that financial disclosure policy, whether regulated or not, should not be overladen with a sense of obligation to restrict disclosure to a particular format designed primarily for a layman's consumption.

Other Sources of Information

Semi-strong efficiency implies that the market absorbs all relevant published information from whatever source. But it does not follow that the corporate report is the principal or even an important source of information to the market. It is conceivable that the same information might previously be obtained by the market from other sources. The conclusion, therefore, is not that corporate reports are essential to the market's efficiency, but that the flow of relevant information is essential whatever the channel of communication. The argument presented here for fuller reporting is, therefore, premised on the assumption that corporate reports provide an authentic source of information to the market.

The Information Content of Security Prices

It has been a common thread throughout the preceding chapters that one of the principal benefits of an efficient market is that it confers reliability on the information signals emitted by the market's security prices. For example, the ordinary investor may safely assume that the price provides a reliable signal of the security's semi-strong worth; the financial manager may assume that prices correctly signal the market's risk-return trade-off in relation to investment evaluation; the accountant may assume that price movements in response to specific accounting data signal the utility of the data's informational content.

More recently, however, it has been shown that the informational signals given by security prices have even wider relevance. For example, it has been demonstrated in a study previously referred to by Beaver, Lambert and Morse[6] that security prices can be used to help predict future earnings. This is something of a reversal of roles, since traditionally it is more customary to view the price of a security as a product of earnings predictions rather than as a basis of predicting earnings. Until recently, research indicated that the most reliable forecast of next year's earnings was the current earnings number adjusted for the market's expected overall shift. That is, despite many elaborate competing models that have been variously tested for their predictive power, the most effective has been the simple one of 'random walk plus a drift'. The 1980 study, however, demonstrated that it is possible to use the price of a share, or more precisely the price-earnings ratio, to improve on the predictive ability of the simple statistical model. Since the size of a firm's price-earnings ratio reflects the market's expectation of the prospective increase in earnings from the current level, then the greater the P/E ratio the greater is the expected rate of growth. If the market is effective at processing information it follows that the relationship of price to current earnings should provide a significant benchmark for predicting future earnings. This is precisely what the tests found, confirming that the growth factor inherent in the P/E ratio furnishes a direct link between the contents of present and future financial reports.

A further example of the informational significance of efficient security pricing is provided by the growing literature concerned with the economic implications of financial disclosure regulation. The object of this literature has been not to test the effect on prices of the information disclosed by the regulation, but to test the economic consequences of the requirement to disclose particular items of information. For example, assuming that the market is truly sensitive to economic changes, then an adverse effect on the security prices of certain companies can be expected to manifest itself on the *announcement* of a new regulation requiring publication of current cost data, if publication is likely to reveal unfavourable insights that were not already perceptible through the historic cost accounts.[7] Similar research has been carried out into the likely consequences of specific accounting regulations for the oil and gas industry, to detect whether adverse effects could be identified with respect to the competitive status of certain firms versus others. Such evidence has in fact been found[8] and has been used by opponents of the regulation to support their case.

It would seem, therefore, that security prices under efficient market conditions are potentially rich sources of information, access to which is restricted only by existing limitations in the researcher's technology.

Costs of Disclosure

It has been stressed that only investors' financial reporting interests have been considered. The existence of other groups for whom the solutions proposed may be totally inappropriate does not directly affect the conclusions drawn since there is no *a priori* reason that a single global solution is necessary or desirable. On the other hand, information production has a cost and there is clearly a limit to which the principles of full disclosure and specific reporting can be implemented.

Preparing a specific report for the market within a decision-input framework carries implications of potentially higher costs, since it implies disclosure, not of one, but of a family of accounting measurement systems to form the raw database for the users' decisions. The traditional philosophy, by contrast, implies a single accounting method and presumably, therefore, a more economic disclosure policy. It is possible that the traditional presumption in favour of a single, all-purpose decision-output approach to reporting is rooted in the belief that there exists an accounting truth which, with the correct methodology, can be elicited from a particular set of data and used to satisfy the needs of virtually all users whatever their specific interest in the company might be. But it is no less likely that the all-purpose approach is accepted as the solution most consistent with cost considerations. Neither conclusion, however, is warranted without considerable empirical support.

Certainly, in the end, it is beyond dispute that information production is an issue for cost-benefit appraisal, but it is far from evident that greater disclosure and special purpose reporting involve material or unwarranted cost.

Conclusion

The traditional notion of the ordinary well-informed layman looking to and depending upon financial reports of listed companies to inform his investment decisions loses much of its significance under efficient market conditions. Most investors can accept prices at their face value. It is the expert professional as price-setter who is the effective user of the related information. This calls for a change in financial reporting philosophy from the traditional emphasis on the primacy of income and position statements to an emphasis on providing financial inputs for the

market to process. It is disclosure rather than accounting method that is
the crucial issue. The ordinary investor benefits from financial reports
not by virtue of what he can read or chooses to read in them, but from the
fact that the reports contain the data needed by the market to establish
prices that approximate to intrinsic worth.

Understandably the proposition that the interests of a significant
group of corporate report users might best be served if given
miscellaneous schedules of financial information without the information necessarily being integrated, or being capable of being integrated,
into an overview of the firm's position, is not one that is likely to be
aesthetically or professionally appealing to most accountants. But this is
a reaction that springs from a long established decision-output tradition
in accounting, in which financial reports were perceived to be incapable
of being wholly useful unless the basic information had undergone a
significant accounting transformation. Such an assumption may in the
end prove for cost reasons to be a valid one, even under efficient market
conditions, but the possibility that it may not is one that should be given
due consideration in any fundamental reappraisal of financial reporting
philosophy.

Notes and References

1. For example, paragraph 24 of the Financial Accounting Standards Board's
   Statement of Financial Accounting Concepts No. 1 identifies potential users
   as 'owners, lenders, suppliers, potential investors and creditors, employees,
   managment, directors, customers, financial analysts and advisers, brokers,
   under-writers, stock exchanges, lawyers, economists, taxing authorities,
   regulatory authorities, legislators, financial press and reporting agencies,
   labour unions, trade associations, business researchers, teachers and
   students and the public'.
2. Whether the directors' view of the firm's state of affairs actually provides
   valid additional information for investment decisions is, of course, a matter
   of dispute. Investment decision theory has long taught that accrual
   accounting concepts, however appropriate for stewardship reporting, are
   irrelevant for the types of economic value decisions made by the market.
3. Financial Accounting Standards Board, (1978) *Statement of Financial
   Accounting Concepts*, No. 1, November, paras 34 and 36.
4. Benston, G.J. (1981) *Investors Use of Financial Accounting Statement
   Numbers: A Review of Evidence from Stock Market Research'*, University of
   Glasgow Press, p.37.

5. Beaver, W., Christie, A. and Griffin, P. (1980) 'The information content of SEC replacement cost disclosures', *Journal of Accounting and Economics*, June.
6. Beaver, W., Lambert, R. and Morse, D. (1980) 'The information content of security prices', *Journal of Accounting and Economics*, March.
7. Beaver, W., Christie, A. and Griffin, P. *op. cit.*
8. Lev, B. (1979) 'The impact of accounting regulation on the stock market: the case of oil and gas companies', *Accounting Review*, July.

10

Conclusion

Market pricing efficiency draws its significance ultimately from its practical implications for market participants, and these have been shown to be potentially far-reaching (Chapters 7–9). Indeed, the concept of pricing efficiency cannot adequately be defined except in terms of its practical consequences for investors, an efficient market being one whose prices are such that investors cannot 'beat the market' other than by chance. Efficiency, therefore, is not a directly observable or intuitively perceptible phenomenon, and the view that one holds on the issue can in the end be derived only from careful analysis of practical attempts to beat the market (Chapters 2, 4 and 5).

These practical consequences make it impossible for investors to be totally neutral on the matter. Neutrality can be supported at the intellectual level only, not at the practical level. It is not necessary to believe that market efficiency is true to justify behaving as if it were true. Those who claim to be uncommitted have to make a choice when faced with practical investment decisions, or remain disinvested. Whatever investment strategy an investor adopts, his effective stance is immediately revealed. If he holds a partially diversified portfolio and transacts frequently, his behaviour effectively places him on the side of inefficiency. If he buys and holds a widely diversified portfolio, he is for practical purposes subscribing to the principles of EMH.

If investors could be assumed to be indifferent to risk, and if it were possible to buy and sell securities without transaction costs, one might expect even intellectually neutral investors to take their chance in the market, and without loss of satisfaction, to trade in inefficiently diversified portfolios in the hope of outperforming the average. But for the risk-averse investor of conventional theory, whose objective is to maximise his return per unit of risk, and who operates in a world where transaction costs are significant, the rational choice is to behave as if the market were efficient until he has grounds for believing otherwise. This, indeed, is the reason why the burden of proof rests on those who claim that the market is inefficient (Chapter 3). A passive buy-and-hold-the-market strategy is, therefore, the logical policy no less for the investor who is unconvinced by the evidence than it is for the investor who is so convinced. In the end, the decision about market efficiency is a personal one. The market is efficient to an individual investor, even when inefficient to others, if such inefficiencies as it contains are imperceptible to him or non-transmittible by those who do perceive them.

Why, then, do so many investors behave as if the market were inefficient for them, if an intellectual assent to the empirical evidence for inefficiency is a rational precondition of such behaviour? Does this not imply that the majority are satisfied with the available evidence? It may do, but it is a reasonable assumption that most have not derived their conviction from a systematic study of the research literature, although the intensity of their conviction may be no less for that. In Chapters 2, 3 and 6 it was argued that casual observation of the market in operation tends to create an illusion of inefficiency and that this illusion, combined with considerable anecdotal support, creates a forceful impression that opportunities for abnormal gain exist and are readily capable of being exploited. From the perspective of most investors, the market appears to be inefficient, and this is apparently enough in practice to make them behave accordingly.

But the practical strategy that investors adopt should depend on more than a vague belief that some opportunities for exceptional profit exist. Recognisable inefficiencies must be shown to exist beyond all reasonable doubt, and their operability must be significant for it to be beneficial for investors to attempt to exploit them. Moreover, efficiency is not a condition which, if diagnosed in a single instance, validates the whole range of activities currently practised by investors who happen to be committed to the notion of market inefficiency. If the market is found to contain a true inefficiency, the rational choice open to investors is not between a passive policy and any of a number of active strategies that are currently offered in the market place, but between a passive policy and the specific investment strategy attested by researchers.

And this indeed is where the crux of the debate lies. If any one or more of the anomalies in the evidence is eventually confirmed to be an authentic inefficiency, then logically good investment theory should incorporate it explicitly into its structure. Investors should accordingly be advised to limit investment to low P/E stocks, or to Value Line securities, or whatever (Chapter 5). But investment theory would then be constructed on the somewhat implausible belief that a market which has been shown beyond all reasonable doubt to be remarkably adaptive and perceptive, is capable of stubbornly refusing to reognise and correct its own proven defects. So, in some extraordinary way, it would continually benefit investors generally to shun large sections of the market portfolio in pursuit of what had been demonstrated to be a source of abnormal profit.

Certainly, if the evidence had suggested that the market was grossly inefficient in its response to new information and offered transparent opportunities for abnormal gain, then it would be quite conceivable that such a market would lack the impetus and urgency to set about eliminating any systematic inefficiencies positively identified by researchers. But the evidence indicates otherwise, namely that if they exist at all, systematic opportunities for exceptional profit are rare and notably inconspicuous. Those who act on the basis that inefficiencies uncovered by research will persist must, therefore, be assumed to found their case on a firm belief in the market's incorrigibility.

However, given the overall view of the market that emerges from the empirical literature, an alternative interpretation is possible, namely that any anomalies periodically shown to exist are either illusions arising from an inadequate modelling of the security pricing process, or, if eventually confirmed to be authentic, are likely to be rapidly consumed away by the competition and dynamism of market forces. It would certainly be surprising even within a substantially efficient market if a few systematic anomalies did not occasionally reveal themselves when the underlying economic relationships are detectable only by relatively new and highly sophisticated statistical techniques. It is, however, important to recognise that market efficiency research is a two-way operation. As the technology becomes more widely known, it is to be expected that the techniques of the researcher will in due course become the tools of the practitioner. The rarer the opportunities for gain, the more intensive will the pursuit of the market's known offerings be, testifying to the existence of a powerful and irreversible tendency for the market's efficiency to increase over time rather than to diminish.

If most investors are incapable personally of directly perceiving market inefficiencies, the issue remains whether it is profitable for them to pursue the recommendations of the expert. Two reasons were presented in the text for believing the contrary. Firstly, the number of successful analysts, if any, who are capable of generating advice which systematically produces a sufficiently high abnormal return to cover transaction costs etc. is evidently a small proportion of the total. It is necessary, therefore, to distinguish the superior analyst from his competitors, and this arguably demands from the ordinary investor no less a level of expertise in performance evaluation than is required from the analyst himself in identifying mispriced securities. Secondly, there is considerable evidence for believing that if the superiority of a particular analyst is rendered clearly visible, the market will price away his recommendations with sufficient speed to prevent his disciples from being able to exploit them systematically.

Therefore, despite the superficial appeal of maintaining a neutral position with respect to the evidence, on the grounds that it is never possible to be certain that an efficient market will not suddenly become inefficient, or that an inefficient market will not become efficient, it is the conclusion of this study that the market can reasonably be classified as near efficient. This is in the sense that the most appropriate practical course of action for the majority of investors is to formulate their investment policies on the basis that the market is and will remain efficient at the semi-strong level, with the consequent implications for financial advisers, financial reporters etc.

Such a conclusion, however, leaves a problem for each individual investor. Near rather than perfect efficiency signifies that all investors fall into one of two classes, those who should benefit from a passive investment strategy, and those who can usefully engage upon an active involvement. How is the individual investor to decide to which class he belongs?

Because near efficiency implies that investment advice cannot be transmitted from perceptive expert to non-expert, then most investors should have little difficulty in recognising their own inaccessibility to the market's price discrepancies. It is the institutional investor currently occupying the role of the expert who faces the more difficult task. To be effective as an active strategist, he must be more than the possessor of a high degree of financial literacy. He must be demonstrably capable of seeing through the prices of securities to their semi-strong worth with sufficient consistency and perception to allow him to earn an economic return for his efforts. And if he is to determine whether he truly is an expert in this sense, it is clear that he cannot depend on the casual self-assessment procedures frequently employed in practice. He must submit to tests no less rigorous than those developed by researchers for evaluating the performance of managed funds. But, as will be shown in the appendix, this is not a simple task, and if it is to be feasible, there is a vital need for existing evaluation techniques to be refined and made more accessible to the individual practitioner.

It is stressed, finally, that the conclusions reached in this study should not be interpreted as grounds for slackening the pace or scope of current research activities. If anything, they underline the need for a regular programme of research to serve the dual purpose of providing a continuing attestation of the market's efficiency and of acting as a monitoring process, so that any short-term imperfections that might occasionally surface can quickly be identified and eliminated. Just as it is in the interests of the general body of investors to know that the market is efficient, so it is in their interests that the market remain so. In addition, there are several aspects of market efficiency that as yet we know little about, not least the process by which the market attains its efficiency, and incorporates the information it receives into its prices. A better understanding of that process could be expected to contribute significantly to both the credibility of the concept of market efficiency and to our knowledge of how best to serve and reinforce its operation.

Appendix

The Assessment of Share Selection Skill

This appendix is concerned with the problems faced by individual investors in finding a suitable yardstick for assessing whether they are capable of effective active investment, in contrast to the great majority of investors for whom a passive strategy appears optimal. The evidence shows that the market's efficiency is enough to prevent anyone other than the most skilled information-processor from seeing beyond market prices to the underlying worth of the securities, at least on the basis of publicly available information. But simply being exceedingly well-informed about financial matters is not enough to ensure success as an active investor, and if individual fund managers etc. are to avoid deluding themselves and others, they must have an effective benchmark for evaluating their selection skills. Certainly, if the general body of empirical research had indicated that the market was highly inefficient, it would be a fair assumption that a sound financial training would provide adequate credentials for an analyst to claim to be able to extract from the market sufficient abnormal profit to justify his fees. The presumption of a minimum degree of effectiveness amongst the analyst profession could reasonably be made by the lay public, as with the products of any other professional training programme.

But when the market is shown to be as efficient as it is, then those who claim to possess superior forecasting ability must be viewed with something of the same degree of scepticism as a statistician who claims to have

159

developed a system for beating the roulette table. The difference, however, is that the latter's claim is more readily testable, since the relevant decisions are simpler, the outcomes more observable, and the time scale more circumscribed.

It must be made clear that the scepticism advocated here is not about whether investment analysts have sufficient knowledge of financial matters, but whether they have a genuine flair for exploiting their knowledge profitably against the market's pricing mechanism. If an individual analyst is shown not to succeed in the latter respect, this is no more a judgment on the adequacy of his financial training than the failure of the statistician to develop a successful system in roulette is a judgment about his statistical expertise. The exercise of comparing the investor's forecasting ability against that of the market is as much a test of the market's degree of efficiency as it is of the investor's skill.

According to the Capital Asset Pricing Model[1] the return expected from any individual risky security is given by the equation:

$$E(R_j) = R_f + (R_m - R_f)\,\beta_j$$

where

$E(R_j)$ = the expected return on security j

R_f = the risk-free rate

R_m = the expected return on the market portfolio

β_j = systematic or non-diversifiable risk

$$= \frac{r_{jm}\,\sigma_j\,\sigma_m}{\sigma_m^2}$$

where

r_{jm} = the correlation between the returns on security j and those of the market portfolio

σ_j = the standard deviations of the returns on j

σ_m = the standard deviation of the returns on the market portfolio

The relationship between individual securities and beta is depicted in Figure A.1, which states that the expected return from a security is an increasing function of its systematic risk.

The implication is that, in an efficient market, every risky asset, to be correctly priced, must be located on the security market line. S, for example, in Figure A.1 represents a mispriced security, since its return is greater than its beta would warrant. If theory is correct, then, any technique designed to measure an individual investor's ability to select

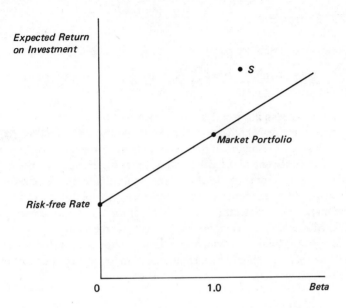

Figure A.1 *Security market line*

mispriced securities should take account of these principles. However, not all performance measures presented in the literature do so. The following four indices indicate the issues involved:

(1) Traditional Index[2]

(Time weighted rate of return)

Excess return $= R_j - R_m$

This measure suffers from the fundamental defect that it ignores risk completely. S in Figure A.1 is more risky than the market portfolio, and it is to be expected that it should earn a higher return. If its excess return is to be judged abnormal, it is necessary to have a yardstick for measuring how much of a higher return is needed to compensate for risk. Otherwise, investors who confine their selections to high-risk securities will appear incorrectly to generate superior returns.

(2) Sharpe Index[3]

(Reward-to-variability ratio)

$$\frac{\text{Risk premium earned}}{\text{Total risk}} = \frac{R_j - R_f}{\sigma_j}$$

The weakness of this index is that it is possible for a security such as S to have a relatively high systematic risk (beta) and a low total risk (σ), or vice versa, and, therefore, if the investor happens to select securities with a bias in either one of these directions, his apparent performance would be misleading. For example, if he chose a portfolio composed of zero-beta securities, that is securities whose movements are totally independent of the market's movements ($r_{jm} = 0$) their appropriate return according to CAPM would be equal to the risk-free rate, yet the securities might have a significant total risk, which, according to the Sharpe Index, would suggest that they should earn significantly more than the risk-free rate.

(3) Treynor Index[4]

(Reward-to-volatility ratio)

$$\frac{\text{Risk premium earned}}{\text{Systematic risk}} = \frac{R_j - R_f}{\beta_j}$$

This measure takes account of the security's covariability with the market, and, therefore, allows a correct ranking of portfolios. Thus if the investor selects S, which has a beta > 1, then his performance ought to be superior to the market's. But the index does not tell us how much the excess should be. Beating the market is not enough; he must beat the market portfolio by more than the amount that the beta of his selected securities would indicate on the security market line.

(4) Jensen Index[5]

(Abnormal performance index)

$$\alpha_j \text{ (Abnormal performance)} = (R_j - R_f) - \beta_j(R_m - R_f)$$
$$= \text{Risk premium} - \text{Risk premium}$$
$$\text{earned} \qquad \text{appropriate}$$
$$\text{under CAPM}$$

This is the only one of the four indices that fully employs the principles of CAPM. α_j will equal 0 if the security lies on SML, otherwise it will indicate the amount of the abnormal return earned by the security. The index can be modified to α_j/β_j to indicate the relative return per unit of systematic risk.

Although the Jensen Index is theoretically the best of the above measures, a number of problems exist with respect to its use in practice:

(a) The Statistical Significance of a Single Investor's Transactions

Obviously chance can account for a positive or negative value of α in individual cases. Because of this, the typical test of investment performance found in the literature tends to include large numbers of security selections made by different experts over a number of years, so that any investors who happen to have a run of good luck are likely to be compensated for by others with corresponding runs of bad luck. This safeguard is more difficult to attain when evaluating an individual investor's performance. Indeed, to produce statistically significant results for an individual, it may be necessary in some cases to cover more years than there are in a typical investment lifetime. Certainly, the initial decision by an investor to engage in an active investment strategy must necessarily be made without sufficient evidence to indicate whether he has the necessary skill. Unless his selections in the first place are laboratory-based he will be committed possibly to years of costly investment activity without any reliable yardstick for assessing whether his efforts are worthwhile.

It has been argued by some writers that an individual investor's performance can be evaluated with statistically significant results from as little as one year's dealing data, provided a sufficient number of individual transactions are included.[6] This assumes, however, that the various share selections are made on the basis of totally independent criteria. For example, if the investor forecasts that the prospective rate of inflation in the year ahead will be less than is generally expected, he will tend to select a portfolio of securities which are known to be highly sensitive to inflation. If his forecast turns out to be correct, then his portfolio will achieve abnormal returns when prices adjust to reflect the actual rate of inflation. But despite the fact that he has appeared to have engaged in a large number of individual transactions, in practice there may be substantially only one event that is being tested—his prediction of the general rate of inflation. Hence, to be confident that the outcome was not simply due to luck in this instance, it would be necessary to study the investor's performance over several years.

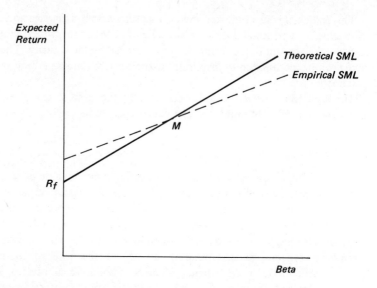

Figure A.2   *Empirical market line*

(b)   Possible Missing Factors

There are theoretical reasons for believing that the classical Capital
Asset Pricing Model is an incomplete representation of the factors that
determine the market's risk-return trade-off. It fails, for example, to
take explicit account of the impact on a security's returns of the differential tax treatment of dividends and capital gains. In addition, the model
has been shown recently to require further refinement to cope with a
measurement bias in favour of smaller firms versus large firms.[7] There
is, therefore, always the possibility that an investor who selects shares on
the basis of a common criterion (such as having a low P/E ratio) may
achieve ostensibly favourable results which are essentially due to
measurement mis-specification.

(c)   The Empirical Evidence

The need for some additional refinement to CAPM before it can be fully
relied upon as a performance yardstick is given support by the empirical
evidence. Although the tests confirm that there is a positive relationship
between expected return and beta, the slope of the security market line is

less than that predicted by the model.[8] Securities with low betas, it seems, tend to earn more than the rate predicted by CAPM, and securities with high betas somewhat less. The relationship between the theoretical SML and the empirical SML is depicted in Figure A.2. It is possible that failure to identify the factors that give rise to this difference could lead to a misinterpretation of observed results.

(d) Implementation Problems

Finally, as already noted in Chapter 5, even if the classic model could be assumed to be perfectly complete, there are problems in applying it in practice, in particular the problem of specifying the market portfolio,[9] which is the world portfolio of all marketable risky assets, not simply the portfolio of listed securities in the investor's domestic market. It is not clear how far failure to identify the precise composition of the market portfolio may lead to some distortion of the results.

Conclusion

The assessment of an individual's share selection skill gives rise to serious problems. It does not appear possible, except perhaps with the aid of elaborate and protracted laboratory-based tests, for an individual to establish himself as a superior analyst without pursuing an active investment policy for several years. The implication is that, unless performance evaluation techniques are improved, the investment community may have to support a significant number of apparently qualified but ineffectual experts to ensure that an adequate pool of truly superior analysts will continue to operate the market's price-setting mechanism effectively. And this indeed is a costly exercise, because it implies that the superior analysts must be able to earn sufficient returns to cover not only their own management costs but those of their less effective colleagues.

Notes and References

1. Sharpe, W. (1964) 'Capital asset prices: a theory of market equilibrium under conditions of risk', *Journal of Finance*, September. See also textbooks such as Brealey, R. and Myers, S. (1981) *Principles of Corporate Finance*, McGraw-Hill.

2. See Cohen, J., Zinberg, E. and Ziekel, A. (1977) *Investment Analysis and Portfolio Management*, Irwin.

3. Sharpe, W. (1966) 'Mutual fund performance', *Journal of Business*, January.

4. Treynor, J. (1965) 'How to rate management of investment funds', *Harvard Business Review*, January.

5. Jensen, M. (1968) 'The performance of mutual funds in the period 1945–64', *Journal of Finance*, May.

6. Dimson, E. and Marsh, P. (1981) 'New approaches to measuring share selection skills', *Investment Analyst*, April.

7. Reinganum, M. (1981a) 'Abnormal returns in small firm portfolios', *Financial Analysts Journal*, March/April.

8. Black, F., Jensen, M. and Scholes, M. (1972) 'The Capital Asset Pricing Model: some empirical tests', in *Studies in the Theory of Capital Markets*, Praeger.

9. Roll, R. (1977) 'A critique of the asset pricing theory's tests, part I: on past and potential testability of the theory', *Journal of Financial Economics*, March.

Questions

1. Does the market have to be perfectly efficient for efficient market theory to have practical validity?
2. Consider some of the problems a researcher is likely to confront in determining whether the market is efficient at the semi-strong level.
3. Why is the market not likely to be particularly efficient at the strong level?
4. Since most investors currently appear to take it for granted that the market is inefficient, is it fair to suggest that the burden of proof is on them to show that EMH is not a valid description of the real world?
5. How would you react to a claim by an experienced investor that he had frequently beaten the market?
6. Is it possible to reach a view about professional investors' capacity to outperform the market without testing every single investor's performance?
7. Consider the view that the verdict on the market's efficiency should be held in suspense until the problems in the research methodology are resolved.
8. To what extent is it valid to conclude that, if market prices are correct, investment ceases to be a skilled activity?
9. If investors are unable to use publicly available information to earn superior returns, does it follow that it is a matter of indifference to them whether relevant information is published or not?
10. Consider the view that, for the purposes of constructing the market portfolio, it is too risky to buy foreign shares unless the foreign country's market has been shown to be efficient.

11. A company is considering raising new finance in the capital market. In what respects should the market's efficiency affect the factors to be considered by management?

12. Indicate the course of action that might be appropriate for an investor who, having accepted the principles of efficient market theory in his investment strategy, is confronted with the findings of a recent research study which allegedly supports the existence of an authentic inefficiency.

Glossary

Active Strategy: An investment strategy where the investor buys and sells securities actively for the purpose of exploiting perceived price discrepancies, and/or holds a portfolio which represents no more than a subset of the market portfolio.

Beta: A statistical measure of an asset's relevant or systematic risk as represented by the covariability of its returns with those of the market portfolio.

Buy-and-Hold Policy: The policy of buying a representative selection of the market portfolio and transacting only to the extent necessary to maintain the balance of the portfolio (also known as passive strategy).

CAPM: The Capital Asset Pricing Model describes the relationship between risk and return in the securities market.

Chartist: An analyst who seeks to predict future price movements from the study of past price movements.

Cost of Capital: The rate of return appropriate in the market to compensate investors for the risk of holding a specific asset or group of assets.

Decision-Input Accounting: A form of accounting where the primary objective is to provide the necessary data for the user to process, without the accounts necessarily attempting to model the user's assumed decision needs.

Decision-Output Accounting: The traditional form of accounting where the objective is to serve users' needs primarily by constructing an integrated model of their assumed decision needs.

Direct Evidence: Evidence relating to market efficiency which focuses on the market's speed and quality (direction and magnitude) of response to specific information items.

Exploitable Inefficiency: An exploitable inefficiency is one which is identifiable, can be authenticated, is material in amount, and is persistent enough to allow investors to profit from it.

Fundamental Analysis: The analysis of publicly available information as a basis for predicting future price movements.

Index Fund: An investment fund which pursues a policy of buying-and-holding the market portfolio.

Indirect Evidence: Evidence relating to market efficiency which focuses on the use of information by experts and their relative success in pursuing an active strategy versus a simply buy-and-hold policy.

Insider: An investor who has access to privileged, price-sensitive information and who exploits his position for investment purposes.

Intrinsic Worth: The best estimate of a security's value in relation to the total set of information available (also known as strong worth).

Market Portfolio: The portfolio of all marketable risky assets in the world in their value-related proportions.

Near Efficiency: The market is near efficient at, say, the semi-strong level if its prices approximate to their semi-strong worth to a degree that makes it unprofitable for any investor other than the very skilled analyst to pursue an active investment strategy using publicly available information.

Passive Strategy: *See* Buy-and-Hold policy.

Perfect Efficiency: The market is perfectly efficient at, say, the semi-strong level if its prices are at all times so close to their semi-strong worth that even the most skilled expert is unable to cover the costs of trading actively on the basis of publicly available information.

Perfect Market: A perfect market is one which, in addition to having a perfectly efficient pricing mechanism, is characterised by perfectly rational investors with equal access to and universal understanding of all relevant information, and where there are no transaction costs or corporate and personal taxation differentials.

Security Market Line: A line indicating the trade-off of risk and return for individual assets.

Semi-Strong Efficiency: The market is efficient at the semi-strong level if security prices adjust rapidly and without bias to all public information.

Semi-Strong Worth: The semi-strong worth of a security is the best possible valuation in relation to the total set of publicly available information.

Strong Efficiency: The market is efficient at the strong level if prices respond rapidly and without bias to all information including unpublished data.

Strong Worth: *See* Intrinsic Worth.

Systematic Risk: Risk that cannot be diversified away.

Technical Analysis: The analysis of past security price movements as a method of predicting future price movements.

Weak Efficiency: The market is efficient at the weak level if it responds rapidly and without bias to the information set contained in the history of past prices.

Bibliography

Alexander, S. (1961) 'Price movements in speculative markets: trends or random walks', *Industrial Management Review*, May.

Ang, J.S. and Pohlman, R.A. (1978) 'A note on the price behaviour of Far Eastern stocks', *Journal of International Business Studies*, Spring/Summer.

Appleyard, A.R., Strong, N. and Walker, M. (1982) 'Mutual fund performance in the context of models of equilibrium capital asset pricing', *Journal of Business Finance and Accounting*, Autumn.

Archibald, T. (1972) 'Stock market reaction to the depreciation switch-back', *Accountancy Review*, January.

Arzac, E. (1977) 'Discussion', *Journal of Finance*, May.

Ball, R. (1978) 'Anomalies in relationships between yields and yield-surrogates', *Journal of Financial Economics*, June/September.

Ball, R. and Brown, P. (1968) 'An empirical evaluation of accounting income numbers', *Journal of Accounting Research*, Autumn.

Beaver, W. (1981) *Financial Reporting: An Accounting Revolution*, Prentice-Hall.

Beaver, W., Christie, A. and Griffin, P. (1980) 'The information content of SEC replacement cost disclosures', *Journal of Accounting and Economics*, June.

Beaver, W., Clarke, R. and Wright, W. (1979) 'The association between unsystematic security returns and the magnitude of the earnings forecast error', *Journal of Accounting Research*, Autumn.

Beaver, W., Lambert, R. and Morse, D. (1980) 'The information content of security prices', *Journal of Accounting and Economics*, March.

Begg, D. (1982) *The Rational Expectations Revolution in Macroeconomics*, Philip Allan.

Belfer, N. (1965) 'Determining the construction of an individual securities portfolio', *Financial Analysts Journal*, May/June.

Benston, G.J. (1981) *Investors Use of Financial Accounting Statement Numbers: A Review of Evidence from Stock Market Research*, University of Glasgow Press.

Bernhard, A. (1975) *Investing in Common Stocks*, Arnold Bernhard and Co.

Bernstein, L.A. (1975) 'In defense of fundamental analysis', *Financial Analysts Journal*, January/February.

Bernstein, L.A. (1978) *Financial Statement Analysis*, Irwin.

Bethlehem, R.W. (1979) 'Reservations concerning the efficient market hypothesis', *Investment Analyst*, September.

Biddle, G. and Joyce, E. (1975) 'Heuristics and biases: their implications for probabilistic inference in auditing', research report submitted to *Research Opportunities in Auditing*, Peat, Marwick, Mitchell & Co.

Black, F. (1973) 'Yes Virginia, there is hope: tests of value line ranking system', *Financial Analysts Journal*, September/October.

Black, F., Jensen, M. and Scholes, M. (1972) 'The Capital Asset Pricing Model: some empirical tests', in *Studies in the Theory of Capital Markets*, Praeger.

Brealey, R. (1969) *An Introduction to Risk and Uncertainty from Common Stocks*, MIT Press.

Brealey, R. and Myers, S.C. (1981) *Principles of Corporate Finance*, McGraw-Hill.

Briloff, A.J. (1974) 'You deserve a break: McDonald's burgers are more palatable than its accounts', *Barron's*, 8 July.

Charest, G. (1978) 'Dividend information, stock returns and market efficiency', *Journal of Financial Economics*, September.

Chiras, D. and Manaster, S. (1978) 'The information content of option prices and a test of market efficiency', *Journal of Financial Economics*, September.

Clarkson, R.S. (1981) 'A market equilibrium model for the management of ordinary share portfolios', Scottish Mutual Assurance Society.

Cohen, J., Zinberg, E. and Ziekel, A. (1977) *Investment Analysis and Portfolio Management*, Irwin.

Collins, D. (1975) 'SEC product-line reporting and market efficiency', *Journal of Financial Economics*, June.

Cooper, R. (1974) 'Efficient capital markets and the quantity theory of money', *Journal of Finance*, June.

Copeland, T.E. and Weston, J.F. (1979) *Financial Theory and Corporate Policy*, Addison Wesley.

Cranshaw, T.E. (1977) 'The evaluation of investment performance', *Journal of Business*, October.

Dann, L., Mayers, D. and Raab, R. (1977) 'Trading rules, large blocks and the speed of adjustment', *Journal of Financial Economics*, January.

Davenport, N. (1975) 'Keynes in the city', in *Essays on John Maynard Keynes*, ed. M. Keynes, Cambridge University Press.

Dennis, G. (1981) 'The current and future role of stockbrokers', *Investment Analyst*, October.

Dimson, E. and March, P. (1981) 'New approaches to measuring share selection skills', *Investment Analyst*, April.

Donnelly, A. (1980) 'Why relative cost is a better basis for investment decisions than the "efficient market" fallacy', *The Chartered Accountant in Australia*, May.

Dreman, D. (1977) *Psychology and the Stock Market*, Amocom.

Dreman, D. (1978) 'Don't go with the pros', *Barron's*, May.

Dryden, M. (1970) 'Filter tests of UK share prices', *Applied Economics*, January.

Dukes, R. (1976) 'An investigation of the effects of expensing research and development costs on security prices', *Proceedings of the Conference on Topical Research in Accounting*, New York University.

Easman, W., Falkenstein, A., Weil, R.L. and Guy, D. (1979) 'The correlation between sustainable income and stock returns', *Financial Analysts Journal*, September/October.

Fama, E. (1965) 'The behaviour of stock market prices', *Journal of Business*, January.

Fama, E. (1970) 'Efficient capital markets: a review of theory and empirical work', *Journal of Finance*, May.

Fama, E. and Blume, M. (1966) 'Filter rules and stock market trading', *Journal of Business, Security Prices: A Supplement*, January.

Fama, E., Fisher, L., Jensen, M. and Roll, R. (1969) 'The adjustment of stock prices to new information', *International Economic Review*, February.

Farber, A. (1976) 'National and international market timing strategies', Commission on Practical Fund Management, 9th Congress, European Federation of Financial Analysts Societies, May.

Financial Accounting Standards Board (1978) *Statement of Financial Accounting Concepts*, No. 1, November, paras. 34 and 36.

Finnerty, J. (1976) 'Insiders and market efficiency', *Journal of Finance*, September.

Firth, M.A. (1972) 'The performance of share recommendations made by investment analysts and the effects on market efficiency', *Journal of Business Finance*, Summer.

Firth, M.A. (1977) 'The investment performance of unit trusts in the period 1965–75', *Journal of Money, Credit and Banking*, Vol. 9.

Foster, G. (1979) 'Briloff and the capital markets', *Journal of Accounting Research*, Spring.

Friend, I., Blume, M. and Crockett, J. (1970) *Mutual Funds and other Institutional Investors, A New Perspective*, McGraw-Hill.

Givoly, D. and Lakonishok, J. (1979) 'The information content of financial analysts' forecasts of earnings: some evidence on semi-strong inefficiency', *Journal of Accounting and Economics*, December.

Glass, R. (1980) letter in *Financial Analysts Journal*, September/October.

Granger, C. and Morgenstern, O. (1963) 'Special analysis of New York Stock Market prices', *Kyklos*.

Grossman, S.J. and Stiglitz, J.E. (1980) 'On the impossibility of information efficient markets', *American Economic Review*, June.

Grubel, H. (1979) 'The Peter principle and the efficient market hypothesis', *Financial Analysts Journal*, November/December.

Hatjoullis, G.S. (1981) 'The efficient markets hypothesis: a critical overview', Working Paper Series, Manchester Business School.

Henfrey, A., Albrecht, B. and Richards, P. (1977) 'The UK stock market and the efficient market model', *Investment Analyst*, September.

Hirshleifer, J. and Riley, J. (1979) 'The analytics of uncertainty and information —an expository survey', *Journal of Economic Literature*, December.

Holloway, C. (1981) 'A note on testing an aggressive investment strategy using value line ranks', *Journal of Finance*, June.

Hong, H., Kaplan, R.S. and Mandelker, G. (1978) 'Pooling vs purchase: the effects of accounting for mergers on stock prices', *Accounting Review*, January.

Jaffe, J. (1974) 'Special information and insider trading', *Journal of Business*, July.

Jensen, M. (1968) 'The performance of mutual funds in the period 1945–64', *Journal of Finance*, May.

Jensen, M. and Bennington, G. (1970) 'Random walks and technical theories: some additional evidence', *Journal of Finance*, May.

Kantor, B. (1979) 'Rational expectations and economic thought', *Journal of Economic Literature*, December.

Kaplan, R.S. and Weil, R.L. (1973) 'Rejoinder to Fisher Black', *Financial Analysts Journal*, July.

Keane, S. (1978) 'The cost of capital as a financial decision tool', *Journal of Business Finance and Accounting*, Autumn.

Keane, S. (1980) *The Efficient Market Hypothesis and the Implications for Financial Reporting*, published by Gee & Co. Ltd for The Institute of Chartered Accountants of Scotland, December.

Kendall, R. (1953) 'The analysis of economic time series, part I: prices', *Journal of the Royal Statistical Society*, Vol. 96, Part I.

Keown, A. and Pinkerton, J. (1981) 'Merger announcements and insider trading activity', *Journal of Finance*, September.

Latané, H. and Young, W. (1969) 'Tests of portfolio building rules', *Journal of Finance*, September.

Lev, B. (1979) 'The impact of accounting regulation on the stock market: the case of oil and gas companies', *Accounting Review*, July.

Levy, H. and Sarnat, M. (1970) 'International diversification of investment portfolios', *American Economic Review*, September.

Lintner, J. (1965) 'Security policies, risk and maximal gains from diversification', *Journal of Finance*, December.

Litzenberger, R.H. and Ramaswamy, K. (1982) 'The effects of dividends on common stock prices: tax effects or information effects?', *Journal of Finance*, May.

Long, J.B. (1981) 'Discussion', *Journal of Finance*, May.

Lorie, J. and Hamilton, M. (1973) *The Stock Market: Theories and Evidence*, Irwin.

Lorie, J. and Nierderhoffer, V. (1968) 'Predictive and statistical properties of insider trading', *Journal of Law and Economics*, April.

Mains, N.E. (1977) 'Risk, the pricing of capital assets, and the evaluation of investment portfolios: comment', *Journal of Business*, July.

Mayers, D. and Rice, E. (1979) 'Measuring portfolio performance and the empirical content of asset pricing models', *Journal of Financial Economics*, March.

Miller, M. (1977) 'Debt and taxes', *Journal of Finance*, May.

Miller, M. and Scholes, M. (1978) 'Dividends and taxes', *Journal of Financial Economics*, No. 6.

Modigliani, F. and Miller, M.H. (1958) 'The cost of capital, corporation finance and the theory of investment', *American Economic Review*, June.

Modigliani, F. and Miller, M.H. (1963) 'Corporate income taxes and the cost of capital: a correction', *American Economic Review*, June.

Murphy, J.M. (1979) 'Second thoughts about the "Efficient Market"', *Fortune*, February.

Murphy, J.M. (1980) 'Why no-one can tell who's winning', *Financial Analysts Journal*, May/June.

Niarchos, N.A. (1972) *The Stock Market in Greece: A Statistical Analysis*, Athens Stock Exchange.

Nicholson, S.F. (1960) 'Price-earnings ratios', *Financial Analysts Journal*, July/August.

Oppenheimer, H. and Schlarbaum, G. (1981) 'Investing with Ben Graham: an *ex ante* test of the efficient markets hypothesis', *Journal of Financial and Quantitative Analysis*, September.

Partington, G.H. (1979) 'The tax-deductibility of interest payments and the weighted average cost of capital: a comment', *Journal of Business Finance*, Spring.

Peasnell, K., Skerratt, L. and Taylor, P. (1979) 'An arbitrage rationale for tests of mutual fund performance', *Journal of Business Finance and Accounting*, Autumn.

Peterson, D. and Rice, M. (1980) 'A note on ambiguity in portfolio performance measures', *Journal of Finance*, December.

Pettit, R. (1972) 'Dividend announcements, security performances and capital market efficiency', *Journal of Finance*, December.

Praetz, P.D. (1969) 'Australian share prices and the random walk hypothesis', *Australian Journal of Statistics*, No. 11.

Reinganum, M. (1981a) 'Abnormal returns in small firm portfolios', *Financial Analysts Journal*, March/April.

Reinganum, M. (1981b) 'Misspecification of capital asset pricing: empirical anomalies based on earnings' yields and market values', *Journal of Financial Economics*, March.

Reinganum, M. (1982) 'A direct test of Roll's conjecture on the firm size effect', *Journal of Finance*, March.

Renwick, F. (1982) 'Discussion paper', *Journal of Finance*, May.

Ro, B.T. (1980) 'The adjustment of security returns to the disclosure of replacement cost accounting information', *Journal of Accounting and Economics*, August.

Roberts, H.V. (1959) 'Stock market "patterns" and financial analysis: methodological suggestions', *Journal of Finance*, March.

Robichek, A. and Myers, S.C. (1966) 'Conceptual problems in the use of risk-adjusted discount rates', *Journal of Finance*, December.

Rogalski, R. and Vinso, J.D. (1977) 'Stock returns, money supply and the direction of causality', *Journal of Finance*, September.

Roll, R. (1977) 'A critique of the asset pricing theory's tests: part 1', *Journal of Financial Economics*, March.

Roll, R. (1979) 'A reply to Mayers and Rice (1979)', *Journal of Financial Economics*, December.

Roll, R. (1981) 'A possible explanation of the small firm effect', *Journal of Finance*, September.

Rosenberg, B. and Rudd, A. (1982) 'Factor related and specific returns of common stocks: serial correlation and market efficiency', *Journal of Finance*, May.

Scholes, M. (1972) 'The market for securities: substitution versus price pressure and the effects of information on share prices', *Journal of Business*, April.

Schwerk, G. (1981) 'The adjustment of stock prices to information about inflation', *Journal of Finance*, March.

Sharpe, W. (1963) 'A simplified model for portfolio analysis', *Management Science*, January.

Sharpe, W. (1964) 'Capital asset prices: a theory of market equilibrium under conditions of risk', *Journal of Finance*, September.

Sharpe, W. (1966) 'Mutual fund performance', *Journal of Business*, January.

Sharpe, W. (1975) 'Are gains likely from market timing?' *Financial Analysts Journal*, March/April.

Sharpe, W. (1981) *Investments*, Prentice-Hall.

Shiller, R. (1981a) 'The use of volatility measures in assessing market efficiency', *Journal of Finance*, May.

Shiller, R. (1981b) 'Do stock prices move too much to be justified by subsequent changes in dividends?' *American Economic Review*, June.

Solnik, B.H. (1973) 'Note on the validity of the random walk for European stock prices', *Journal of Finance*, December.

Sunder, S. (1973) 'Relationships between accounting changes and stock prices: problems of measurement and some empirical evidence', *Empirical Research in Accounting: Selected Studies*.

Thompson, A.P. (1981) 'Inflation accounting has helped share selection', *Investment Analyst*, October.

Treynor, J. (1965) 'How to rate management of investment funds', *Harvard Business Review*, January.

Umstead, D. (1977) 'Forecasting stock market prices', *Journal of Finance*, May.

Van Horne, J. (1980) *Financial Management and Policy*, Prentice-Hall.

Ward, C. and Saunders, A. (1976) 'UK unit trust performance 1964–74', *Journal of Business Finance and Accounting*, Winter.

Watts, R.L. (1978) 'Systematic abnormal returns after quarterly earnings announcements', *Journal of Financial Economics*, September.

Waud, R. (1970) 'Public interpretation of Federal Reserve discount rate changes: evidence on the announcement effect', *Econometrica*, March.

Weston, J.F. and Brigham, E. (1981) *Managerial Finance*, Holt-Saunders.

Whitcomb, D. (1977) 'Discussion', *Journal of Finance*, May.

Whittington, G. (1979) 'Beware efficient markets theory', *Accountants Magazine*, August.

Williamson, J. (1972) 'Measuring mutual fund performance', *Financial Analysts Journal*, November/December.

Working, H. (1934) 'A random difference series for use in the analysis of time series', *Journal of the American Statistical Association*, March.

Author Index

Subject Index